CONTENTS

The arrangement follows the ancient division of Durham into

Cover: **Durham from the north-west.**
              Royston Thomas.

THE PENINSULA

The Fortress Site

The historic city of Durham perches precariously on a narrow neck of land below the commanding north wall of the Castle, seat of the prince-bishops whose bishopric stretched from the River Tees to the Scottish Border. East of the old city, an upper reach of the River Wear is crossed by Elvet Bridge, while to the west, Framwellgate Bridge spans a lower stretch. Between these bridges the river flows in a deep gorge almost surrounding the Peninsula whose high, south-sloping plateau is crowned by the great romanesque Cathedral.

When the Congregation of St Cuthbert arrived in 995, they may have taken the steep route followed by Saddler Street where, in 1974, excavations behind the shops on the west side revealed the remains of a succession of circular wattle buildings with hearths, dating from the 10th century. The Congregation chose the higher site, which could be made impregnable, to settle and build the first church to enshrine the body of their saint. The escarpments and river formed natural defences, the only access being from the north.

The sides of the gorge were originally perpendicular as they remain below St Oswald's, where the ancient burial ground has been respected. Elsewhere, they have been quarried extensively, yielding an estimated 80,000 tons of stone to build the Cathedral, monastic buildings, Castle and

The fortress site from the south-west: the Cathedral and monastic buildings to the south rise within the Norman defence walls. *Claughton Photography.*

fortifications. Geologists calculate that 68,200 tons were needed in the Cathedral itself. The stress on the underlying sandstone is only one-third of the stress which would cause failure.

Early earth and timber fortifications withstood the siege of Malcolm, King of Scots, in 1006. About 1038 his successor, King Duncan, also besieged the site unsuccessfully when the citizens sallied forth and slew many Scots.

After the Norman Conquest, William I found a pretext for displacing the Saxon bishop Aegelwine. He was replaced in 1071 by Walcher of Liège (Lorraine), whose friend Waltheof, Earl of Northumberland, was responsible for the building of the nucleus of the present Castle, although there is evidence of an earlier structure. It became the seat of military, civil and ecclesiastical power from which the bishops of Durham reigned as princes in a buffer state between England and Scotland.

Fortifications

Walls still surrounding the Peninsula augmented the natural defences from an early date. When they were strengthened in the 12th century, an inner wall was erected connecting the Castle keep with the Cathedral choir. The northern entrance at the head of Saddler Street was guarded by a gate-tower with a portcullis. Bishop Langley rebuilt it in 1417 and it became the county prison until 1819. It was demolished in 1820 as an obstruction to carriages.

Parts of the high wall and bastion tower of about 1400 connecting the North Gate and Castle keep are visible near the top of Saddler Street. The street line continues the whole length of the Peninsula in the North and South Baileys, some of whose original houses abutted the outer fortification walls. They were tenanted by bishops' men in return for Castle defence. From Saddler Street, Owengate leads to Palace Green. A handsome Tudor black and white house stands close to the site of the gate through the inner bailey wall. Nearby in the Castle the bishops' mint issued royal currency.

The Prince-Bishops and their Palace

Palace Green (formerly 'the Place') lies between the Cathedral and the Castle which was also the bishops' palace. Formerly bishops' property within the Castle's outer walls, Palace Green is surrounded by buildings once closely connected with their activities as churchmen, civil administrators and benefactors. Houses covered it until the 12th century, but were removed as pollution risks and fire hazards. Occupants not directly attached to Cathedral or Castle were settled on the site around the present Market Place. When, through the munificence of Bishop and Cathedral Chapter the University was founded, Palace Green was envisaged as its quadrangle. The Castle was handed over to the University, the bishops henceforth using Auckland Castle as their only residence. The University accommodated the episcopal courts, offices and almshouses in new buildings nearby.

The Castle

Durham Castle: the Courtyard and entrance to the Great Hall. The Castle, former residence of the Prince-bishops, is now University College, the oldest college of the university, and is available for holidays and conferences during university vacations. Guided tours during Easter and summer vacations, Mon-Sat 10 a.m. to 12 noon, Sundays 2-4.30 p.m.; closed Christmas vacations. Adult £2·50, children £1·50, family ticket £6. (Tel: (0191) 374 3863. Fax: (0191) 374 7470.)   *Claughton Photography.*

The Castle gateway, approached across the former dry moat, is Norman; but its exterior was faced in the 18th century by James Wyatt, whose 'restorations' scar both Cathedral and Castle. Massive 16th-century doors, of solid oak and iron, are still closed at night, when the entrance is only by the wicket gate.

Since 1836, Durham Castle has housed University College, the earliest college in Durham University which was founded in 1832. The bishops retain the use of the state apartments and H.M. judges lodged here during the assizes until 1972.

The Castle began to subside and major restoration work, including piling to stabilize the ground, was undertaken in the 1920s with assistance from the Pilgrim Trust. In 1995 an appeal fund was opened to meet the heavy costs of modern restoration and maintenance.

Castle Gateway from Palace Green.
Claughton Photography.

Courtyard and Norman Chapel

A spacious courtyard is enclosed by buildings of various periods in pleasing harmony. A crypt below the courtyard on the north-east is early Norman. At the lowest level of the east-west range, the Norman undercroft chapel of 1072, originally entered by a newel stair at the south-west, has a nave and two aisles. Plain round pillars of local sandstone with naturally decorative markings support plain groined vaulting. The square abaci of the capitals are carved with grotesque masklike faces, figures and animals, no two being alike. Part of the herring-bone pavement is probably original. The windows are round-headed; but those on the north, originally 6 inches in width, were widened and the splays increased in 1840. Neglected by later bishops and used as a passage by the early University, it was restored for worship in 1952.

Modern repair and maintenance work in the Castle has been attended by archaeological investigation. Recent discoveries have included an 11th-century oubliette and in the courtyard, part of the early bishops' lodgings.

The North Range

After a disastrous fire in Silver Street damaged the Castle in the 12th century, Bishop Hugh of Le Puiset built opposite the gateway a lower hall for dining and an upper hall for the constable, responsible for the soldiers, armour and horse of the bishops' army. This, known as the Norman Gallery, was modernised on the outside in the 18th century, but retains window arcades in triplets, with chevron mouldings, inside on the south and west. The matching south-east doorway opens on to a newel stair to the lower hall, which was divided into several rooms by Bishop Tunstal (1530–59). Of these, the bishops' dining-room, now the senior common room, has a contemporary

Castle Courtyard looking east to the Keep; left: the Clock Tower and exterior of Bishop Tunstal's chapel.
Claughton Photography.

panelled ceiling. The fine senate room fireplace with 17th-century armorials probably originated in the Exchequer.

Bishop Tunstal's Gallery and Chapel

Bishop Tunstal built a gallery on the south front of this lower hall to connect his new chapel on the east with the great hall on the west, destroying the earlier first-floor entrance stair from the courtyard, but leaving the magnificent late Norman doorway in the gallery. The chapel, of 1542, has carved return stalls brought from his chapel at Auckland Castle in 1547, and a 17th-century west screen made for Bishop Cosin whose arms it bears. Bishop Crewe (1674–1721) extended the chapel eastwards but reinstated the original window. The organ in the gallery incorporates some of the pipes and the choir organ case of a 'Father' Smith organ built on the Cathedral screen in 1683, and dismantled in 1872. It was restored in 1921.

The Castle: Bishop Tunstal's chapel.
Durham County Council.

The Great Hall

West of the courtyard, a new great hall was built in the late 13th century over the Norman undercroft. Enlarged in about 1350, it had a musicians' gallery and two thrones symbolising the bishop's two roles as prince of church and state. Bishop Fox (1494–1501) reduced the hall to its former length, removing the lower throne and gallery. The two stone pulpits may have been intended for trumpeters. Butteries and pantries occupy the space saved; and beyond, a great kitchen, still used, was formed from Bishop Hugh of Le Puiset's south-west tower by inserting windows and three huge fireplaces. The motto *Est Deo gracia* and the date 1499 are carved on the oak buttery hatch with Bishop Fox's badge, which appears also on the screen between hall and pantries. The device, a 'pelican in her piety' drawing blood from her breast to feed her young, symbolises Christ feeding his Church in the Holy Communion. The present elegant screen and gallery date from 1887. Portraits of University founders and benefactors and the north stained glass window inserted to commemorate its Jubilee are reminders that this is the dining hall of University College.

The Castle, as church property, was confiscated during the Commonwealth and suffered during ownership by the Lord Mayor of London. After the Restoration in 1660, Bishop Cosin carried out extensive repairs, building the neo-classical portico before the great hall doorway and the tower with the elaborately carved black staircase (1665) at the north end to connect the floors of the Norman wing. The late medieval keep became ruinous and was replaced by a replica in 1840 to contain undergraduates' rooms.

Palace Green

West side

Leaving the Castle, the wall on the right shelters the Fellows' Garden, once a private retreat for the bishops, adjoining the older University Library buildings which occupy the west side of Palace Green up to Windy Gap, site of the Windishole Postern. The University's main library is at the corner of South Road, in a new building begun in 1982 (*see page 20*).

Nearest the Castle gate, Bishop Neville's Exchequer Building of about 1450 housed various judicial courts. Beneath lièrne vaulting and the remains of a newel stair, two doors admit to separate parts of the court room which now contains the Sharp Library of early printed books from Bamburgh Castle. The room above houses Dr Routh's large library of rare books from Magdalen College, Oxford.

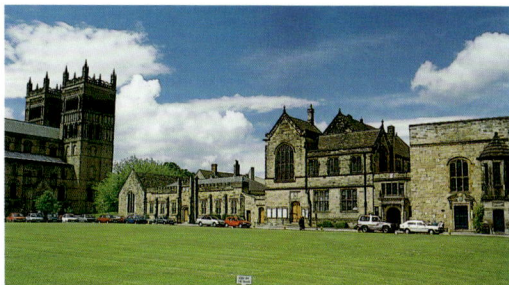

Palace Green: west side (left to right), Old Grammar School, old Registry and University Library.
Claughton Photography.

Next is the library founded in 1669 by Bishop Cosin for both clergy and the literate public. Its treasures include his annotated copy of *The Book of Common Prayer* of 1611 with suggestions for the revision of 1662. In 1834 the University added a gallery with a separate entrance by a tower stair from Palace Green for undergraduate use.

The former Diocesan Registry beside Windy Gap was erected in 1820 after the removal of the Assize Courts rebuilt by Bishop Cosin in 1664. Windy Gap leads to the river banks alongside the Dean and Chapter's old Grammar School (*see also page 17*),

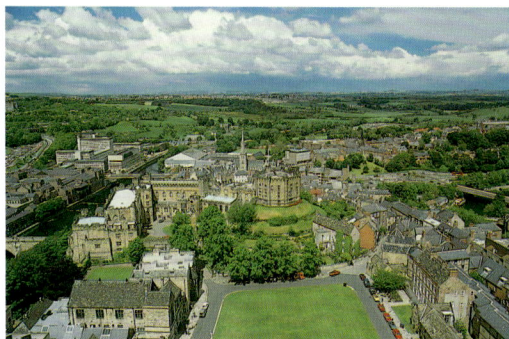

Palace Green from the Cathedral tower: east side with the head of Owengate, Bishop Cosin's Hall and old almshouses (1666). The Castle motte, surmounted by the keep, guards Saddler Street below. *Claughton Photography.*

built in 1661 and now the University's Music Department. Annexed to it and facing the Cathedral is the former Divinity House, once the residence of J. Meade Falkner, Cathedral Librarian 1921–32, novelist and author of *The Lost Stradivarius*. The tall cross commemorates Alfred Tucker, appointed Bishop of East Equatorial Africa in 1890 straight from his curacy at St Nicholas.

East side

Crossing obliquely to the east side of Palace Green, the new Bishop Cosin's Almshouses of 1838 stand at the top of Owengate; and the 17th-century house with a magnificent door-head, formerly Archdeacon's Inn, is Bishop Cosin's Hall so-named from use by a University hall of that name between 1851 and 1864. Bishop Cosin's original almshouse building of 1666 is next door. It accommodated four men and four women, with schools in the north and south ends, one for grammar and one for writing and plainsong, refoundations of schools of Bishop Langley (1406–37). The University converted it to lecture rooms (later linked with the adjoining neo-gothic Pemberton building). It is now the Almshouse Café and Restaurant.

On the corner, Abbey House with its Queen Anne front earlier faced south. Its ancient blocked doorway is close to the site of another gate in the inner bailey wall at the head of Lygate (*lich* – corpse) beside the Cathedral graveyard. Lygate became Dun Cow Lane after the 18th-century renewal of the carving, high on the Cathedral's north face. It represents the legend, first recorded in the late 16th century, of a woman calling her dun cow directing the Congregation of St Cuthbert to the Peninsula.

Dun Cow Lane leading from the North Bailey to Palace Green.
Claughton Photography.

The Cathedral

St Cuthbert

The young Cuthbert, noble and attractive, saw a vision on the night of St Aidan's death in 652 and next day went to Melrose to enter its monastery. Soon, at Ripon, he became guest-master but, with Celtic training, fell foul of Wilfred and Roman practices. Returning to Melrose he became Prior, was transferred to Lindisfarne (Holy Island) in 664 and became Bishop in 684. He died in 687 on his beloved island of Inner Farne and was buried in Lindisfarne Priory. His stone coffin was opened twelve years later, revealing his body fresh as in life. A miracle was proclaimed and the body, transferred to an oak casket, was venerated.

Flight from Holy Island

In danger from Danish raiders, the Congregation of St Cuthbert, descendants of the earlier community, left Lindisfarne in 875 and, with their wives, children and cattle, began the 'wanderings' over the north. Among their treasures they took with them the elaborately carved oak casket which had two partitions. In the lower lay St Cuthbert's body with the bones of St Aidan and other saints, and St Oswald's head. The upper part held valuable manuscripts, including the Lindisfarne Gospels now in the British Museum, and the related Durham Gospels, still in Durham. The Congregation with its bishop settled at Chester-le-Street in 882; but further danger in 995 sent them to Ripon and finally to Durham.

Here they built a temporary wooden shrine, south of the present Cathedral, to protect their treasures, followed by a 'White Church' of stone with east and west towers and a shrine for St Cuthbert's relics. The graves of the early Congregation, men, women and children, were found during 19th-century restoration of the chapter house and four of the cross-heads discovered with them are on display.

Perhaps for political reasons, as their lands were hereditary, the Congregation of St Cuthbert was ejected under William I. Bishop Walcher of Lorraine (1071–80) planned monastic buildings, traces of which are incorporated in the south-east corner of the cloister and include a wide branched staircase, now broken, and the deanery and refectory undercrofts. The introduction of Benedictine monks led to the growth of the legend that St Cuthbert disliked women.

The present church

In 1093, Bishop Walcher's successor, Bishop William of St Calais or Carilef (1081–96) demolished the 'White Church' to build a new Cathedral with its south wall 30 ft north of the north wall of its predecessor. It had apsidal (rounded) ends to choir and aisles in the manner inspired during his exile in Normandy during 1088–91. An architectural adventure, this is the earliest example in north-west Europe of a church planned to be roofed entirely by stone-ribbed vaulting. By 1104 the eastern end was finished except for the north transept, which was vaulted by 1110. Under Bishop Rannulf Flambard (1099–1128) the nave was completed except for the vaulting, which the monks achieved during the next five years when the see was vacant. The main church was finished in 1133. The compound piers of the nave alternate with circular columns, whose girth equals the height from base to capital (22 ft), in matching pairs of chevron, diaper and spiral designs, deeply incised. The massive stones, quarried locally, were brought to the church carved ready for erection. The style of the wall-arcading of interlaced arches was

The Cathedral: view from the central tower looking to the western towers and South Street, with the river and weir to the left.
Claughton Photography.

probably first used in Durham, while the transverse arches supporting the nave vaulting are probably the earliest pointed arches in England. The interior was painted with brilliant colours and designs, of which a restored example may be seen on the south wall of the nave.

The Galilee

After an attempt to add an eastern chapel, unsuccessful because of unstable ground, Bishop Hugh of Le Puiset (1153–95) added the Galilee to the west end in about 1175. This chapel covered the Cathedral's western forecourt and severed the double fortification wall to the south (still intact) from the wall-passage running north to the Castle. Its well, rediscovered in March 1896, had an outer dip-well for public use (*see page 22*) whose overflow later formed St Cuthbert's Well on the banks below.

The Galilee roof is supported by slender Purbeck marble pillars augmented by stone columns. In 1414, Bishop Langley added his chantry and altar tomb during his lifetime, blocking the great west door and providing two side doors into the nave.

The alcove to the north contained the Holy Cross altar where 12th-century wall-paintings of a bishop and a knight flanking looped curtains are probably associated with Bishop Hugh of Le Puiset as builder of the Galilee and with the donor of the relics of the cross once displayed in a central niche, now blocked, behind the modern cross. Nineteenth-century writers identified them with St Cuthbert and St Oswald. To the south is the tomb of the Venerable Bede. His bones were brought from Jarrow to Durham by Aelfred the Sacrist about 1022 and transferred from the feretory (behind the high altar) to the Galilee in 1366/7.

Ancient sanctuary

After the Galilee was built, the north door of the nave became the Cathedral's main entrance. Internally this doorway remains as it was built in the time of Bishop Geoffrey Rufus (1133–40) with its outer arch ornamented by foliage and eighteen diamond-shaped medallions, some depicting animals or birds, others illustrating lively scenes from real life or legend: a man whips a boy lying over a stool while holding up his dress; two people embrace; a long-robed and bearded man strangles with a rope another wearing a knee length garment; two show centaurs with conical helmets shooting with bows and arrows.

When this doorway was created it was entered through a stately porch (later enhanced by buttresses). From two chambers above, reached by stairs descending from the triforium, monks kept watch day and night for any fugitive seeking sanctuary, by grasping and knocking with the ring in the mouth of the bronze lion's head on the door below. Enamelled or glazed eyes must once have emphasized its grotesque appearance. The sanctuary seeker was admitted immediately and the Galilee bell rung in the north-west tower.

He was allowed 37 days' refuge, with food, drink, and bedding in a grated enclosure beneath the dormitory night stairs between the south door and the Galilee door. Clad in a black cloth gown, with

Durham Cathdral: Sanctuary Knocker on the North door.
Claughton Photography.

St Cuthbert's cross in yellow on the left shoulder, he was safe within the sanctuary of church and churchyard until he received royal pardon, or came to terms with his accusers. If neither happened, he was required to forfeit his goods and abjure the realm, walking in his distinctive robe to the nearest port carrying a wooden cross. Three hundred and thirty-one men claimed the sanctuary of St Cuthbert between 1464 and 1524, and the privilege continued until James I's reign.

The outer porch, with its chambers above, was demolished by James Wyatt, who reduced the doorway to its present appearance with the outer decoration shaved off and recarved.

The original 12th-century 'sanctuary knocker' suffered corrosion caused by industrial fall-out pollution. It was removed for conservation at the British Museum where a bronze replica was cast and in 1980 replaced the original, which is now displayed in the Treasury.

Chapel of the Nine Altars

In the 13th century, with improved building techniques, the Nine Altars' chapel was achieved at the east end. (As Benedictine monks were ordained priests, each celebrating mass daily, many altars were needed.) In its north transept a statue of Bishop William Van Mildert (1826–36) commemorates the last prince-bishop, co-founder of the University and donor of the Castle.

The Shrine

From the Nine Altars' chapel, steps lead to a raised platform behind the high altar. Here was the medieval feretory, where relics were kept. In the centre stood the richly decorated shrine of St Cuthbert, visited by innumerable pilgrims. Its treasures were removed by Henry VIII's commissioners in 1537. Today the saint's remains lie

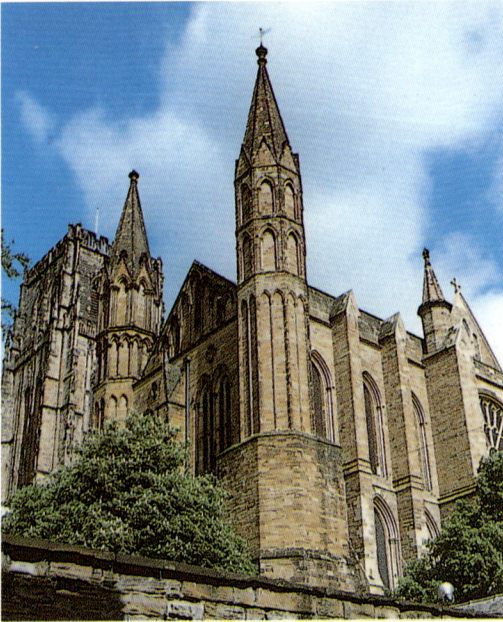

The Cathedral: Chapel of the Nine Altars. *G. Dresser.*

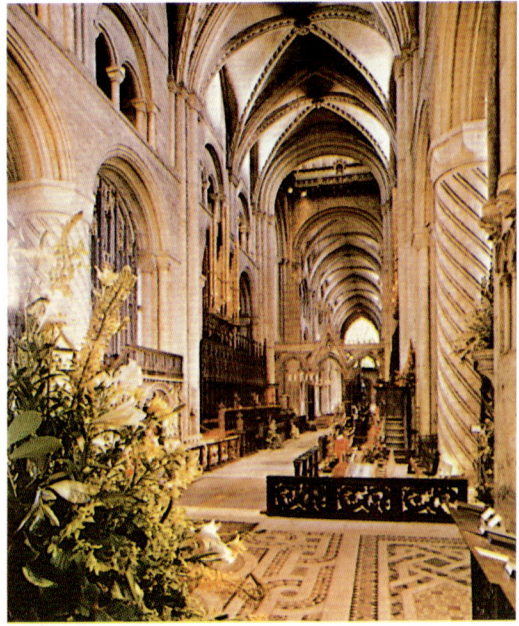

Durham Cathedral: the choir from the north-east corner of the sanctuary, showing, on the south side, Bishop Hatfield's tomb and the bishops' throne above, built 1345–81, and the highest in Christendom; the 17th-century choir stalls beneath elaborate tabernacle work; the triforium and clerestory of the choir (1093–6); and the high choir vault of *c.* 1250. Beyond the choir screen stretches the nave, 205 ft long, whose high vaulting, completed before 1133, probably has the earliest transverse pointed arches in England. *Ian Curry.*

beneath a simple inscribed slab marked by four tall candlesticks, designed by Sir Ninian Comper, as was the tester, depicting Christ in Glory surrounded by the symbols of the four Evangelists. It hangs from the four holes in the vault above from which once hung the painted and gilded shrine cover. The semi-circular white line shows the site of the apse, the original east end of the Norman church.

The Choir

The delicate altar screen, partly paid for by John, Lord Neville, between 1372 and 1380, was brought from Caen in Normandy. The bishops' throne, the highest in Christendom, was erected by Bishop Hatfield (1345–81) whose tomb is beneath. Scottish royalist soldiers imprisoned in the Cathedral after their defeat by Cromwell at the Battle of Dunbar in 1640, destroyed the woodwork except for the elaborate clock of about 1500 in the south transept. Bishop Cosin inspired the style of the pinnacled choir stalls which replaced the lost medieval stalls in 1665. Their return stalls and matching screen, with its 'Father' Smith organ built in 1683, were removed when Sir Gilbert Scott designed the present screen (1870–6). The west face of the 17th-century screen, partly reconstructed in the south-west aisle, is markedly different in style; and matching choir aisle doors have been reused to lead to the Castle buttery. The early (romanesque) screen was solid stone; two of its sculptured panels are displayed in the Treasury.

Cloister, Precincts and Library

The remains of the medieval Benedictine monastery to the south are the most complete in England. The cloister garth, surrounded by alleys once protected by glazed windows, has its well and the basin from the monks' lavatorium (washing place) formerly opposite the refectory door. The north alley, against the church, enclosed part of the monastic library and study alcoves. On the eastern alley is the chapter house, completed by Bishop Rufus (1133–40) containing the graves of early bishops. Above the slype or passage connecting it with the south transept Prior Wessington (1416–46) built a room to which he moved the library from the cloister. South of the cloister the Norman refectory, derelict after the dissolution, was converted by Dean Sudbury, about 1684, into the Dean and Chapter Library. To the library was added in 1854 the immense dormitory, built 1396–1404 and spanned by complete oak trees. The library totals over 50,000 volumes including about 360 volumes of medieval manuscripts, some of Bede's time from Jarrow and Wearmouth.

Durham Cathedral: the cloisters, looking south-west, with the refectory, left, and dormitory, right; the lavatorium basin, centre, has been moved from the south-west corner. *Claughton Photography.*

The Priory Kitchen

The old doorway next to the refectory entrance has been re-opened to give access to the vast octagonal Priory Kitchen built in the 14th century by the master mason John Lewin. It has six great fire-places and intricate vaulting to support a central louvre to expel fumes. It served as the kitchen for the Deanery until 1940 and was connected with it by a long rising passage (since demolished) built against the south wall of the refectory. Later it housed thousands of Priory and Cathedral documents dating from the 11th century onwards, and administered in co-operation with the University. In 1992 they were moved to No. 5, The College, making it possible to use the Priory Kitchen as the Cathedral bookshop from 1997.

The College, north-west view: left to right, The Priory Kitchen and offices, Refectory, and Durham Light Infantry Memorial Garden. *Claughton Photography.*

Undercrofts and Treasury

In the undercroft beneath the dormitory the south end, formerly cellars for the adjacent great kitchen, is now a restaurant, while the north part, once the monks' common room, is now the Treasury. Here St Cuthbert's 'coffin', portable altar and cross, with Anglo-Saxon embroidery, manuscripts and other treasures are displayed for visitors.

From the south-east corner of the cloister a passage, probably 17th-century, leads to the College or Cathedral Close. Within the passage, opposite doors lead to two exhibitions: in the refectory undercroft (right) built c. 1080, is now *Building the church*, an imaginative display designed for school children (access by appointment only); the contemporary undercroft to the Prior's Hall (left) houses *Cuthbert yesterday and today: an audio-visual of the living Cathedral* (18 minutes), with superb photography. (For opening hours, which vary according to season, see notice board at north door of Cathedral.)

The College (Cathedral Close)

Continue down the passage to the College. During the Commonwealth, Oliver Cromwell arranged to found a university here. Staff were appointed but no students were enrolled.

The Deanery abuts the refectory and incorporates 11th-century work and the medieval priors' hall. Opposite is the Durham Light Infantry memorial garden, sheltered by the refectory's south wall and the octagonal 14th-century Priory Kitchen.

The steep 'dark entry' leads west to the river banks beneath the sub-dean's house where the early

The College (Cathedral Close): Water Tower from the Cathedral Chorister School entrance.
Claughton Photography.

Norman vaulted undercroft of the guest-house survives. Adjacent houses, set back, surmount the infirmary undercroft, while Georgian-style houses to the south are conversions from monastic out-buildings. The 18th-century tower was a reservoir for water, piped across the river from medieval times.

Beside the gateway of c. 1500 is a medieval lane spanned by an early timber-framed granary, leading to gylehouse (where gyle or wort, an infusion of malt, was fermented to make beer), brewhouse, and bakehouse.

South Bailey

Just outside the gates was the monastery's almonry school whose Master, also Master of St Mary Magdalene Hospital, controlled the almonry where the children slept and four old women lived (24, North Bailey). In the other direction the South Bailey had its own parish church of St Mary-the-Less,

St Mary-the-Less, former parish church of the South Bailey, is the burial place of members of the Bowes family, and now the College chapel of St John's College. *Claughton Photography.*

South Bailey: the College gateway, with the former St Helen's chapel above the arch. *Claughton Photography.*

now the chapel of St John's College. Although rebuilt in the 19th century, it contains Norman work, including a sculpture from St Giles in the chancel, and Elizabethan woodwork. Near the organ is a wall memorial to the dwarf Count Boruwlaski.

The bailey houses gradually became gentlemen's residences with gardens stretching to the east bailey wall and below to the river. Typical is 'Bowes House', 4, South Bailey, now part of St John's College. Occupants and history can be traced from medieval times. Owned in 1452 by the Master of Kepier Hospital, it had access to the monastic cellarers' orchard beyond the wall. Later occupants included the widow of Dean Whittingham, translator of the Geneva Bible (quoted by Shakespeare), the Bowes family in the 17th and 18th centuries (ancestors of the Queen), the Liddells (whose descendant was 'Alice in Wonderland') and many famous clergy. The reception room has a delicate 18th-century plaster ceiling. South Bailey descends to the Water Gate which superseded the medieval gate in 1778. The wall on the right retains its sentry walk, while on the left, guard towers stand sentinel at intervals to Kingsgate.

North Bailey

Returning to the North Bailey, some houses are reputedly haunted: an elegant lady and Almonry children (no. 23); a musician (no. 24); and a crooked man in black breeches, ruffled shirt and nightcap emerging from a cellar.

St Chad's College, on the corner of Bow Lane, faces the Cathedral. Part of its hall, built in 1961, replaced a quaint bow-windowed house where the gifted Porter family lived before leaving for Edinburgh in 1780. Jane (1776–1850) wrote *The Scottish Chiefs* (1810), a novel with Durham references; Robert (1777–1842), who became Sir Robert Ker Porter, author and painter of historical panoramas, married a Russian princess; and Anna Maria (1780–1832) who published *Artless Tales* in 1793. Prince Leopold read her *Knight of St John* to Princess Charlotte on the eve of her death (1817).

Bow Lane leads to the site of the Kingsgate postern and ford, traditionally associated with William the Conqueror's flight. Supposedly, he was seized with dread after an attempted opening of St Cuthbert's coffin to challenge the belief that the body was incorrupt, mounted his horse and galloped, non-stop, terrified to draw rein until over the Tees into Yorkshire and safe from the saint's power. In the 15th century Bow Bridge crossed the river here. Today, the Kingsgate footbridge leads to Dunelm House and Elvet; and steps, formerly a grassy vennel, down to the riverside path, emphasise the impregnability of the strong walls above the steep slopes. Bow Lane has views of Hatfield College whose main gates and chapel (1853) are in North Bailey, and the fine 18th-century house with handsome portico and panelled interior. The College nucleus is the mid-18th-century 'Red Lion' coaching inn, whose elegant dining-room, once assembly rooms, has a Venetian window. In 1827 Durham had about 18 daily coaches and 41 carriers before railways caused the business to decline. Alongside the lane, St Mary-le-Bow's south wall was part of the inner bailey wall whose gateway (or 'bow') crossing North Bailey, was annexed to the church. Both fell in 1637. Church rebuilding was completed in 1685 and the tower *c.* 1702. Within is good contemporary woodwork. Closed in 1967, it was converted to a heritage centre in 1976.

The cottage next the churchyard hides timber-framing; and north of Hatfield College gates is 'Jevons' which replaces the Georgian house of John Gulley (1783–1863), champion prize-fighter of England in 1806. On the left, Bailey House covers the site of a Maison Dieu and Museum Square up to Dons' Passage. On Owengate corner the University's Law Department occupies the former Halmote Court office (closed in 1952). After removal from Palace Green in 1855, Durham's Chancery Court continued to function here and contained the judicial seat from the bishops' Exchequer Building.

Bow Lane: looking from the site of the Kingsgate postern to the Cathedral. The 18th-century porch spanning the pavement protected ladies alighting from carriages in bad weather before the introduction of umbrellas.

Claughton Photography.

BOROUGH OF DURHAM & FRAMWELLGATE

The borough of Durham, below the north walls of the Castle, was one of six separately administered areas (the boroughs of Durham, Crossgate, Gilligate and Elvet, Elvet barony, and St Mary Magdalene) now within the modern city. It comprised only the Market Place, Saddler Street and Silver Street with the addition of the suburbs of Claypath and Framwellgate from an early date.

Saddler Street

Saddler Street descends steeply from the Peninsula to the Market Place. After the demolition of the North Gate at the street head in 1820, a subscription library and assembly rooms were built. The latter, now the Salvation Army Citadel, has fluted pillars similar to those of the two shop-fronts beside Drury Lane lower down. Across this vennel, so-called by 1754, the former robe-makers' shop masks the foyer of an 18th-century theatre whose auditorium sloped to a stage below. The street had several theatres, including two opposite, opened in 1771 and 1791. Here, Stephen Kemble engaged actors such as his sister Mrs Siddons (1755–1831).

The street between Magdalene Steps (leading to Elvet Bridge) and the Market Place was formerly

Saddler Street on Miners' Gala Day: a miners' lodge banner passing Magdalene Steps in the procession to Elvet in the 1950s. (*See also page 21.*)　　　*Margot Johnson.*

named Fleshergate and occupied by butchers (flesh-hewers). Mrs Clemens' famous Durham mustard was probably first ground at a mill behind no. 73 in the 17th century. The business descended to Ainsleys and was bought by Colman's c. 1900.

The street retains a number of Tudor properties. The best example of a merchant's house is no. 79. The timber-framed structure and attic fireplace may be 14th-century and a fine 17th-century staircase connects the four storeys. 'Neptune' heads, roses, fleurs-de-lys, pomegranates and thistles decorate its elaborate and priceless second-floor plaster ceiling of about 1560.

Elvet Bridge

Magdalene Steps lead from Fleshergate (used as the shambles until the 19th century) to Elvet Bridge. Approximately two-thirds of the bridge are in St Nicholas parish, the remainder being in Elvet. A slab of blue marble formerly marked the boundary between the two. (*See page 21, column 2, for an account of St Andrew's chapel at the Elvet end of the bridge.*)

It has ten arches (fourteen according to Leland in the 16th century) and was built by Bishop Hugh of Le Puiset (1153–95), reconstructed c. 1228, repaired extensively under Bishop Fox (1494–1501) and again in 1601. Before 1400, shops and houses were built on the ends of the bridge, and the spaces under the dry or land arches were leased out for storage. The great flood of 1771 destroyed three arches, but refuges (alcoves for pedestrian safety) remained until 1804–5 when the bridge's width was doubled and the low vennel (formerly reached down steps) on the north-west was covered.

A medieval gate formerly pierced the city wall, the remains of which are now hidden by shops in the former Souterpeth (shoemakers' street). The mayor met James I in 1617 at the north-west bridge tower beside the 13th-century St James' chapel, founded by Lewin, a Durham burgess. Both tower and chapel have long vanished.

The chapel was replaced in 1632 by the House of Correction. Its former workhouse, repaired in 1715 to be used with the woollen manufactory in the Market Place, is part of the shop next to the post-1820 archway on the south side of the bridge and two floors below the modern street level. The House of Correction and its workhouse were connected by a passage bridging the old low vennel, with steps descending from a high doorway in the bridge arch which is now visible. A lower doorway leads to the two cells remaining below the bridge on the north side. Here, Jimmy Allen, champion of the Northumbrian pipes and piper to the Duchess of Northumberland, was imprisoned for horse-stealing. Pardon came the day after his death. His ghostly piping is said to haunt the cells remaining beneath the bridge. Other cells remain beneath adjacent shops.

The Market Place

From the Market Place, Silver Street, now pedestrianised, descends westwards to Framwellgate

Bridge and the suburbs of Framwellgate and Crossgate; while Claypath leads north-east to Gilesgate from the east end of St Nicholas' church. Here stood the Clayport Gate, demolished in 1791, which passed through walls running east and west beside Paradise Lane and Walkergate (both destroyed) which connected fords of the Wear just south of the modern Leazes Road roundabout and Millburngate Bridge.

Remains of these walls, built about 1314 by the burgesses after Scottish raids, lie beneath shops on the east side of the Market Place.

The medieval Market Place, where a weekly Saturday market still flourishes, was dominated by St Nicholas' church with its churchyard, the Tolbooth, and the Pant. It was extended c. 1841 by the paving of St Nicholas' churchyard where the Tanners' Guild traded.

Guilds affiliated to the 15th-century Corpus Christi Guild, whose guildhall stood behind Claypath, once controlled trade and commerce and linger on today. Market tolls were collected in the Tolbooth, where the bishops' bailiff held a fortnightly court in a room above shops and stalls, until Bishop Tunstal built a stone Guildhall on the west side of the Market Place. In his time the marble sanctuary cross from Gilesgate was moved here. This was replaced for James I's visit in 1617 by one with a lead roof and twelve-pillared arcade, subsequently demolished. Its stone was used to build a nine-arched piazza south of St Nicholas' churchyard in 1780.

The Pant provided the only public well from 1450, with water piped across the river to supply Bacon Place, on the east side of the Market Place, the town house of Thomas Billingham of Crook Hall. The well-head, surmounted from 1729 by Neptune, renewed in 1863 and 1900, remained until 1920. The statue of Neptune was removed to Wharton Park (above the railway station) but was badly damaged

there. It was repaired and refurbished to grace the Market Place again from May 1991. Neptune is associated with an 18th-century scheme, never implemented, to make the Wear navigable up-river as far as Durham, to promote industry and commerce.

The Market Place: north side, with St Nicholas' church, and (left) the Town Hall. The equestrian statue of the 3rd Marquess of Londonderry in hussar uniform, is the finest work of Raffaelle Monti (1818–81), executed for Durham in 1858 and erected in 1861. From the church, Claypath leads (right) to Gilesgate. *Claughton Photography.*

Town Hall and Guild Hall

An equestrian statue of the 3rd Marquess of Londonderry (*see page 31*), in hussar uniform, stands in front of the Town Hall steps. It is the finest work of Raffaelle Monti (1818–81).

When the city's business outgrew the old Guildhall, a new Town Hall was erected to the rear and opened on 29th January, 1851. In the sixty feet long entrance corridor is a copy of Bishop Hugh of Le Puiset's charter to the burgesses in 1179. The original is preserved in the County Record Office with those of Bishop Pilkington (1565), Bishop Matthew (1602), Bishop Crewe (1685) and Bishop Egerton (1780). Bishop Crewe gave most of the present civic plate, hall-marked 1672–95, as the corporation had misappropriated its early silver.

Showcases contain the clothes and violin of 'Count' Boruwlaski, a Polish dwarf 39 inches tall, who published his *Memoirs* and music of his own composition. After extensive travels he came to England in 1782. He spent the last years of his life in Durham and was a friend of the Ebdons. Thomas Ebdon, the composer, was Cathedral organist from

Elvet Bridge connecting Elvet with the historic borough of Durham and its Market Place. From Brown's boat-house, right, rowing boats may be hired, and the pleasure cruiser the *Prince Bishop* takes visitors beyond Prebends' Bridge. *Claughton Photography.*

1763 until his death in 1811. (He is remembered today for some of his church music, and especially for the evening canticles of his Service in C.) The Misses Ebdon kept house for Boruwlaski at a cottage, now demolished, below 12, South Bailey, near Count's Corner, where he died in 1837 in his late nineties. (*See also page 22.*)

The Town Hall, seventy-two feet long and thirty-six feet wide, was designed by P. C. Hardwicke of London with a fine hammer-beam roof, fifty-six feet to the ridge, to imitate that of Westminster Hall, a reminder that the ancient bishops' courts were modelled on those of Westminster.

The decor represents the city's history. Twelve angels terminating the roof beams, and shields within the quatrefoils in the spandrils of the arched beams, display the coats of arms of its sixteen incorporated trade guilds. Over the Prudhoe stone fireplace are the arms of Bishop Maltby (1835–56) impaled with those of the See; and flanking panels record the men who fell in World War I (1914–18), and the city's honorary freemen. High wainscotting bears the names and dates of mayors, chaplains, and town clerks since the 1835 Municipal Corporation Act, when the bishops' Palatinate jurisdiction was transferred to the Crown. The coats of arms of leading county families embellish the upper walls and panels below the west window. Its top lights display the arms of Allan of Blackwell, Shipperdson of Durham, Wharton of Dryburn, and the architect; side lights represent bishops who gave charters to the city: Hugh of Le Puiset, James Pilkington, Tobias Matthew and Nathaniel Crewe; the lowest panels show Edward III, with his barons, thanking the citizens for their loyalty; and three central lights depict the medieval guilds' annual procession to the Cathedral on Corpus Christi day bearing banners and torches as they were affiliated to the Corpus Christi guild founded by Bishop Langley (1406–37).

Their mystery plays are lost, but fine guild silver survives, and some guild records, including the Dyers and Litzters Book are preserved.

The Guildhall (left of the entrance corridor) was built by Bishop Tunstall in 1535 to replace one associated with St Nicholas in 1316. After damage during the 1640 Scottish invasion, Bishop Cosin rebuilt it in 1665. Major alterations in 1752 were soon followed by refacing and possibly rebuilding; but the oak fittings and carved coats of arms are Cosin's. On the walls hang guild coats of arms, painted in 1783–85. One represents the Merchant Company (1561) comprising Grocers (1345), Mercers (1393), Salters (1394), Ironmongers (1464), and Haberdashers (1487). Ten others represent the Cordwainers [workers in Cordova leather or shoemakers] (1430); Skinners (1327) joined by the Glovers (1638); Weavers (1450); the Drapers and Tailors (1549); the Butchers (1520); the Blacksmiths, Lorimers [makers of spurs and bits], Locksmiths, Cutlers and Bladesmiths (1610); Free Masons, Rough Masons, Wallers, Slaters, Paviours, Plaisterers and Bricklayers (1410–11); Carpenters, Joiners, Coopers, Wheelwrights and Sawyers (1571); Barber Chirurgeons, Ropers and Stringers (1468); and Goldsmiths, Plumbers, Pewterers, Potters, Painters and Glaziers (1532). The Dyers became extinct in 1811 when the last member died. These guilds played an important part in civic life until 1835, when their principal rights were removed. Several surviving guilds still meet here.

The adjacent Mayor's Chamber was panelled by George Bowes, MP, in 1752, doubled in size in 1848–49 and altered in 1890. Its magnificent fireplace was presented by Walter Scruton, Clerk of the Peace, when he sold to the University the building now Hatfield College. He took out the fireplace, but removed from the overmantel portraits of Charles I and Queen Henrietta Maria, now replaced by reproductions.

Framwellgate Bridge, below the Castle, crosses the river from the junction of South Street, Crossgate, Millburngate and North Road, and leads to steep Silver Street and the Market Place. *Claughton Photography.*

13

The Burlison Art Gallery, right of the corridor, and above part of the Market Hall, is named after its chief benefactor, Clement Burlison (1830–99), a local landscape painter.

This is the site of **New Place**, town residence of the Nevilles of Raby and Earls of Westmorland, whose gardens sloped down to the river. The Crown confiscated the property in 1569 after the rebellion of the northern earls. Henry Smith's Charity bought it from James II for use as a school, cloth manufactory, and St Nicholas Parish workhouse. The buildings were demolished in 1852 and rebuilt as they stand today. In 1926 Durham Corporation bought the whole site, including that of the Town Hall.

St Nicholas' Church

In 1283 Archbishop Wickwane fled down steps at the west end of St Nicholas' church to Kepier Hospital after a rebellious reception at Durham Priory.

St Nicholas', whose Norman north wall once continued the city wall, became unsafe after alterations. It was rebuilt in 1858 to a neo-gothic design by J. F. Pritchett. 'Jesu, lover of my soul' was first sung to J. B. Dykes' well-known tune at the re-opening. The church was modernised in 1981.

Claypath

Much of the ancient Claypath has vanished. To the left, at the foot of the former Walkergate (or cloth-workers' street) stood Henderson's factory which succeeded the woollen industry of St Nicholas' workhouse. William Henderson pulled down Shakelock Hall (which superseded an earlier mansion) c. 1840 to extend his works. Mackays, makers of the famous Durham carpets, followed Henderson and recently moved their factory to Dragonville on the eastern outskirts.

On the east side of Claypath behind shops is the neglected Quaker burial ground and the site of the Bluecoat School. Opposite, the Independent Chapel of 1751 is hidden behind the neo-gothic Congregational church of c. 1888, now the United Reformed church.

Leazes Place, in Regency style, was built, surprisingly, in 1843–6. It leads to Leazes House, erected for William Henderson c. 1847, which Durham High School held 1887–1968 and which Durham University now owns.

Providence Row, next to the General Post Office, leads to the riverside. Here the Sands, greensward stretching to Kepier Hospital, is the Freemen's common pasture and the site of a traditional Holy Week fair. On the slope above, St Nicholas' 'new' churchyard adjoins the site of St Thomas' chapel, whose burial ground, approached by a lane from Claypath, was used as late as the plague year of 1597. Near the Sands, below Millburngate Bridge, the burgesses ground their corn at the Bishops' Mill, recorded in Boldon Book (1183), rebuilt in the 17th century and demolished in 1972. The mill race later served an adjacent ice rink. Between this and the site of the Clock Mill, opposite, the dam and weir deepen the water, providing extra defence for the Castle.

Returning to Claypath, Bakehouse Lane, where stood a medieval common bakehouse, leads to Mayorswell field, named from the Maire family, former owners. Robert and Grace Maire became

Roman Catholics after seeing men of that faith hanged at Gibbet Knowle, Dryburn, in 1591.

Tinklers' Passage, opposite, leading towards the river, formed the boundary of St Nicholas' parish, once marked also by a medieval leaden cross standing in the roadway. From here, Gilesgate rises to a modern roundabout and beyond it, Gilesgate Green, centre of a formerly separate settlement.

Silver Street and Framwellgate Bridge

Silver Street, descending to Framwellgate Bridge, is now pedestrianised. Of its former timber-framed houses only three remain, two on the north side. In 1964, the fine house of Sir John Duck (d. 1691) was demolished, its black oak staircase was rescued by Bowes Museum, Barnard Castle, and a panel painting depicting Duck's story was saved by Alderman Luke. When Duck was an unemployed apprentice, a raven dropped a gold sovereign at his feet and his fortune changed. He became master-butcher, mayor, keel, ship and mine owner, founder of Lumley almshouses, and Sir John Duck of Haswell-on-the-Hill.

Two steep vennels or alleys join Moatside Lane which skirts the Castle motte. A medieval Maison Dieu or hospice continued above the lower vennel until the 17th century.

Bishop Flambard, whose competence as William II's tax collector gained him the bishopric, built Framwellgate Bridge about 1120. After damage by flood in 1401, it was rebuilt using tolls from a temporary ferry and money from the Prior and Convent and Bishop Langley (1406–37). The Castle's Norman gallery immediately overlooks it; towers and gates defended each end; and a postern led to the river banks. Increasing traffic caused removal of the Silver Street gate in 1760, the battlements in 1828, and early 19th-century bridge widening. (*See also The Banks, page 22.*)

Framwellgate

Across the bridge, Crossgate lies to the left and Framwellgate to the right. The boundary between was the Mill Burn, now in a conduit beneath North Road, which was opened as King Street in 1831, William IV's coronation year.

Framwellgate was reached formerly through Millburngate, which survives only as a footway beside a timber-framed house at the entrance to Millburngate shopping centre. Here, steps descend to the riverside near the site of two mills, where the Mill Burn cascades from a pipe into the river beside the weir. A path joins the road beneath Millburngate Bridge and beside Millburngate House (modern government buildings) to Crook Hall, which may be reached also via Framwellgate and Sidegate.

The prosperous merchants' houses of Framwellgate became 19th-century slums and were demolished, except for an 18th-century town house with beautiful plasterwork c. 1741. Today, it overlooks Millburngate roundabout. Once the Wheatsheaf Inn, it became a convent, later an Arts Centre, and is now occupied by Disc Training.

Beside it, ancient Castle Chare, now a modern road, climbs steeply to the station past St Godric's

Roman Catholic church, built for Irish workers who moved here in the 19th century. It was restored after serious fire damage in 1984.

Crook Hall and Sidegate

Crook Hall (a private house) overlooks the river where waterside steps led to a ferry to the Sands within living memory. The boat was worked from a cable across the river.

The site, occupied before 1217, was part of the manor of Sidegate. The 14th-century manor house was probably built by Peter del Croke. The solar wing is ruined, but the hall, open to the roof, survives with minstrels' gallery and screens passage. Here lived Joan del Croke, who married John de Copeland. He captured King David of Scotland at Beau Repaire (Bearpark) when northern armies routed the Scots at the Battle of Neville's Cross in 1346, afterwards being knighted and made constable of Roxburgh. He and Joan held Crook Hall until 1362 when he became Keeper of Berwick.

The Billinghams lived here c. 1390–1667, altering the west end and creating from the earlier buttery and pantry a winter parlour whose timbers bear coloured designs. From it leads a primitive wooden stair, said to be haunted by a white lady – a Billingham.

John, called the Cowherd of Billingham, married Bishop Kellaw's sister in 1248, founding a prominent local family. Thomas Billingham, when piping water from his Fram Well to his town house, granted to the Corpus Christi Guild a supply for the Market Place Pant in 1450. In 1636 Cuthbert Billingham cut the pipes to divert water to his mills at Crook Hall, but was forced to restore them. They provided the city's main supply until c. 1850. An earlier Cuthbert Billingham, a founder, c. 1464, of the Silver Street Maison Dieu for poor travellers, accompanied Robert Lumley the hermit on pilgrimage overseas.

The Mickletons altered Crook Hall further in 1671 building westwards a gabled extension. James Mickleton, a lawyer, began to collect valuable local records known as the Mickleton-Spearman manuscripts and now in the University Library.

The Hoppers of Shincliffe added the westernmost brick three-storey wing of 1736, farm buildings and the handsome granary attached to the higher of the two mills. A bird carrying a hopper or basket decorates the first-floor drawing-room ceiling, perhaps referring to their name. Their most distinguished tenant was the Reverend James Raine (1791–1858), Durham's indefatigable historian. His son James, the York historian, was Chancellor of York Minster; and his daughter Annie (Mrs Raine-Ellis) edited Fanny Burney's diaries, wrote a novel about late Georgian Durham clergy families, and copied designs from Cathedral Library illuminated manuscripts for Ruskin. He, like Wordsworth and Boruwlaski, visited Crook Hall. The restoration in 1983–4 of the hall and the Mickleton wing by John and Mary Hawgood, the former owners until November 1995, received a Civil Trust Commendation. Keith Bell, the present owner, is carrying out further restoration. Visitors may be admitted occasionally (0191) 384 8028.

From Crook Hall lane, Sidegate climbs to the railway arch. Beside it stands the medieval Fram Well head, its opening sealed and with an inscribed notice of the Pant Masters, officers of St Nicholas' parish.

Field footpaths lead to a farm enclosed from the bishops' park of Frankland, which today gives its name to a new prison.

Crook Hall: the south front, showing the Mickleton wing (right), built 1671 and the three-storey Hopper addition of 1736. The climbing pear trees are probably over 200 years old.   *M. R. Hawgood.*

D. L. I. Museum and Arts Centre.

Aykleyheads, Dryburn and North Road

The main road to Chester-le-Street and Newcastle passes through the railway arch. An unobtrusive left turning leads to Wharton Park, given by W. Lloyd Wharton about 1850, which has tennis courts and affords spectacular views. In a garden setting on the right, the Durham Light Infantry Museum and Arts Centre offers changing exhibitions and concerts.

Left of the road junction, St Cuthbert's (Anglican) church occupies the site of the medieval St Leonard's hospital, probably where St Godric's sister died. Across the roundabout is Dryburn Hospital. Between them was Gibbet Knowle where Edmund Duke, Richard Holyday, John Hogge, and Richard Hill, seminary priests, were executed in 1591. Their bravery so impressed Robert Maire of Hardwick and his young bride Grace Smith, who were present, that they became Roman Catholics. Grace, the only daughter of Henry Smith and niece of John Heath of Kepier, was disinherited by her father, who left his fortune to found Smith's charity. (*See also page 14 under Claypath for the Maire family.*) It was said that a brook near the gallows ceased to flow at the time of the execution; but the name Dryburn is older.

John Boaste, another recusant priest, was executed on 24th July 1594. These priests were among the forty English martyrs canonized by Pope Paul VI on 25th October 1970.

On the right is County Hall. In its spacious entrance, where modern friezes illustrate Durham history, the County Record Office displays documents. Return to Framwellgate Bridge may be made down tree-shaded North Road. Parallel, at a higher level, is Western Hill, with the obelisk erected by W. L. Wharton in 1850 to mark the meridian 1,200 yards north of the University's observatory. North Road passes the County Hospital (opened 1853). Nearby is Waddington Street United Reformed church and the Miners' Hall in grounds off Redhills Lane; while a little way beyond, in Hawthorn Terrace, the world famous organ factory of Harrison and Harrison has flourished since 1872. Across the North Road roundabout are the neo-classical North Road Methodist church and the bus station. Shops line the road to Framwellgate Bridge, dominated by the Castle.

CROSSGATE or THE OLD BOROUGH

Crossgate, called the Old Borough to distinguish it from the monks' new borough of Elvet created in the 12th century, was separately administered as the priors' manor. It comprised Allergate, inhabited in the 12th century, Crossgate itself (the direct road west before North Road existed) and South Street, which climbs high above the west bank of the Wear and leads south.

St Margaret's Church

The church of St Margaret of Antioch, at the junction of Crossgate and South Street, was founded as a chapel in St Oswald's parish to serve Crossgate and Framwellgate. Increasing population necessitated the creation of separate parishes in the 19th and 20th centuries. Gracious, but heavily restored, it retains the south nave arcade and western portions of the building of c. 1150. The chancel was extended eastwards and the north arcade built c. 1195, the tower rebuilt in the 14th century, and the south aisle in the 15th century. Squints beside the chancel arch afford views of the high altar from north and south aisles, that to the south being cleverly contrived so that the south aisle altar is seen also from the nave. Sir John Duck (*see also page 14*) lies buried in the central aisle. An orchard in South Street and the adjacent site of the priory's fishponds became extensions to the churchyard in 1820 and 1825.

Below the church, timber-framing from a demolished house remains in the end of the Fighting Cocks, a reminder of cock fighting. Steps ascend to high footpaths in Crossgate, where 17th-century façades cloak older structures. The manorial Tolbooth was on the north side below Allergate. Crossgate continues past the former St Margaret's Hospital to a crossroads, where the Peth leads to the suburb of Neville's Cross and the cross, now a mere stump, commemorating the battle of 1346.

St Margaret of Antioch: founded as a chapel in the parish of St Oswald, served as the church of both Crossgate and Framwellgate until new parishes were formed in the 19th and 20th centuries because of increasing population (*see also page 18, col.1*). Members of the Billingham family of Crook Hall are buried here.   *Claughton Photography.*

South Street, Pimlico and Durham School

From St Margaret's church and the public library South Street climbs alongside the river. Picturesque houses face views of Cathedral and Castle acclaimed the finest in Europe. At the top once stood a cross, the priors' prison (abandoned in the 13th century) and their dove cote. A stile leads to riverside paths and Prebends' Bridge.

In nearby Pimlico is 'The Grove', once the home of Stephen Kemble, the actor who played Falstaff before George IV without padding. Opposite is the Bellasis, so-named from its 13th-century tenants and now the site of Durham School. At Bellasys House (Sir) William Fothergill Cooke (1806–79), son of a Durham doctor, helped Professor Wheatstone develop the 5-needle electric (railway) telegraph patented in 1837. (S. F. B. Morse is believed to have invented his electro-magnetic telegraph in 1835.)

In 1842, Bellasis passed from the Cookes to Durham School, transferred there from Palace Green to buildings designed by Salvin (1844). The impressive chapel (1924–6) is a 1914–18 war memorial. The school's King's scholarships date from Henry VIII's new foundation.

Along a leafy lane and past school playing fields a roundabout is reached. Below, a private road through the White Gates leads to Prebends' Bridge. Opposite is Quarry Heads Lane and to the right Potters Bank alongside the boundary between Crossgate and Elvet. Bearing left from Potters Bank are St Mary's College, St Aidan's College, the Oriental Museum and Van Mildert College.

South Street head: once the busy centre of the Old Borough of Crossgate, dreams high above the river gorge.
Claughton Photography.

THE BOROUGH OF GILESGATE and ST MARY MAGDALENE

Gilesgate and St Mary Magdalene

Gilesgate may be reached from Claypath or Leazes Road. From the footbridge at the roundabout a panoramic view includes, to the west, the 1857 Victoria railway viaduct crossing North Road, County Hall, Aykleyheads, the Durham Light Infantry Museum and Crook Hall below. To the east the motorway link road follows the old railway track from the first Durham station, whose buildings overlook the roundabout. When Durham graduate Edward Bradley (as 'Cuthbert Bede') based his novel *Verdant Green* on the early university, an illustration for the first edition showed undergraduates with luggage in Gilesgate nearby. Opposite stands the ruined chapel of St Mary Magdalene, consecrated in 1451 and transferred from a nearby unsatisfactory site. Its inmates, under a Master from Durham Priory's Almonry, were aged poor of the vicinity. Until the 17th century it was the church of an extra-parochial district, which was transferred to St Nicholas' parish in 1978, although the ruins remain extra-parochial. The graveyard became a garden in 1822.

College of St Hild and St Bede

Near the footbridge is the College of St Hild and St Bede, together with the University's department of education. Formerly two diocesan teacher-training colleges, St Hild's was founded in 1858 for women and St Bede's for men, begun in Framwellgate in 1841, and moved here in 1846–7. Its chapel (1938–9) was designed by Seely and Paget.

Up the hill is Gilesgate green and St Giles' church overlooking Pelaw Woods and Old Durham, where the Tempests built a new manor house which the Londonderrys inherited, but abandoned in the 18th century. Its terraced gardens overlooking the river

Kepier Hospital: the gateway from the riverside path near the ruined mill. The barns to the left, later encased in stone and brick, are timber-framed, and had new roof timbers about 1450. *Claughton Photography.*

and Maiden Castle became a mid-19th-century pleasure garden. (*For a detailed account see pages 30–32.*)

St Giles' Church and Kepier Hospital

St Giles' church, founded as the chapel of Bishop Flambard's hospital of 1112, where St Godric held a minor lay office, retains its original north nave wall. During the troubles of 1144, the buildings were burnt and the present church is substantially 13th–15th-century rebuilding. In the sanctuary, an oak effigy commemorates John Heath (*d.* 1591), Warden of the Fleet Prison, who purchased the dissolved Kepier Hospital property, including Old Durham manor. (*See also pages 30–32.*)

ELVET

Elvet is probably Aelfet-ee (Swan Island) where Peohtwine was consecrated Bishop of Whithorn in Galloway, once part of Northumbria, in 762.

In monastic times, Elvet was administered by Durham Priory's hostillar, who held manorial courts here, and was responsible for the furnishing and fabric of the parish church. The extensive parish then included all the land outside the loop of the river, with the chapelries of St Margaret's, Witton Gilbert, and Croxdale (now separate parishes), besides Finchale Priory, where the present congregation of St Oswald's still holds an annual Ascension Day evening Communion service in the ruined church.

The ancient parish was probably a large Anglo-Saxon estate.

A footpath near St Mary Magdalene descends to Kepier Hospital to which St Giles' Hospital, for a Master and thirteen brethren, moved in about 1180. (It may be reached also from the Sands.) They relieved the poor, welcomed pilgrims and entertained visitors, including Archbishop Wickwane (1283), Edward I (1298) and Queen Isabella (1312). The gateway is 14th-century and Kepier Farm is mostly 14th-century work on 12th-century foundations. Its west wall incorporates a stone crucifix and the east windows have original tracery. John, son of the first John Heath, built a mansion adjoining the southern medieval buildings. The remaining loggia is the only one of its period in the county.

St Oswald's Church

The dedication is to St Oswald, who became a Christian during his exile with his brother and sister on Iona, in the monastery founded by Columba. Later, as King of Northumbria, reigning from Bamburgh, he invited St Aidan from Iona to settle on Lindisfarne (Holy Island) and found there a monastery from which to send missionaries to convert his extensive kingdom to the Christian faith. Many early dedications to St Oswald reflect the work of St Aidan and his immediate successors. King Oswald died in 642 fighting Penda, pagan King of Mercia, at Maserfield near Oswestry. His severed head was later placed in St Cuthbert's coffin, now in Durham Cathedral.

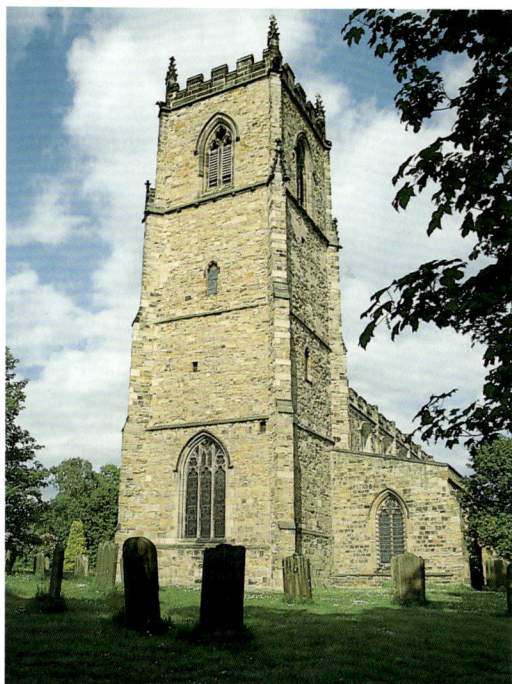

St Oswald's Church: Its western tower stands close to the riverside footpath from the ancient churchyard to Prebends' Bridge. *Claughton Photography.*

The church's chancel arch and the four eastern bays of the nave are of *c.* 1195, and survive a 14th-century rebuilding of both chancel and north aisle. The fine chancel stalls, clerestory, and tower are 15th-century work. Subsidence, once thought to be due to Elvet Colliery working, but caused by walls built over earlier burials, led to the restorations of 1834, 1864, and 1883. (Although coal seams lie below the church, they are too thin to work.) The chancel and south aisle walls, which had recesses for recumbent effigies, were rebuilt. A fine pre-Reformation roof with painted panels was also lost. Its wooden corbels carved into grotesque heads still remain.

In 1864 a delicately hued west window by Ford Madox Brown (associate of William Morris) was inserted in the tower. It depicts the life of St Oswald from the time of his baptism on Iona.

The tower stairs, a straight flight rising in the thickness of its south wall, use twenty-four reversed 13th–14th-century grave covers. Their carved designs may be seen overhead on ascending the steps to the belfry. Some incorporate swords (gentry) or occupational symbols: e.g. a horn on a cord (a forester); a mattock (a husbandman); a hatchet (a woodcutter).

Anglo-Saxon sculptured stones, parts of crosses used later as building blocks by medieval builders, were found in the tower's west wall and in the churchyard wall bordering Church Street, suggesting a pre-Conquest church here before the Community of St Cuthbert settled on the Durham peninsula. These sculptures are displayed in the dormitory of Durham Cathedral.

The vicar from 1862 to 1874 was John Bacchus Dykes, the hymn writer. He named his familiar tune to 'Jesu, lover of my soul', 'Hollingside'. He lived at Hollingside cottage, near Hollingside Wood in the parish, near the University's Botanic Garden. He is buried in the graveyard opposite the church.

Two wall tablets are of special interest. At the east end of the south aisle, an oval memorial commemorates George Smith of Burn Hall (*see pages 42–44*), son of the Reverend John Smith, canon of Durham and editor of a scholarly edition of Bede's *Historic Works*. George Smith who bought Burn Hall (in the parish) in 1717, was a Non-juror (one who refused the Oath of Allegiance to William and Mary) who took holy orders in the Non-juring church and became its titular Bishop of Durham. He died in 1756. The other notable wall tablet is the exceptionally fine Elizabethan memorial at the east end of the north aisle, commemorating Christopher Chaytor of Butterby, in the chapelry of Croxdale, who died in 1592, aged 98.

A dowsing survey, carried out in 1982, showed the plan of an earlier church. It had an eastern apse and

St Oswald's Church: the west window, by William Morris and Co. tells the story of St Oswald and his relics: baptism, coronation, sending missionaries, Cadwallon's death, slaying of King Oswald, his body enshrined. The coats of arms are in memory of John Fogg-Elliot, of Elvet Hill, d. 1881, one of the Twenty-Four for forty years and churchwarden.

Margot Johnson.

St Oswald's Church: looking west to the organ and tower arch.
P. D. Collins.

a shorter nave flanked by north and south porticuses (side-chambers of Anglo-Saxon type). At the west end, within the present nave's fifth bay, a square structure may have been a tower or narthex. At this point the round pillars of the later nave continue with octagonal ones making two further bays.

In July 1983, the installation of a new heating system provided opportunity for limited archaeological excavations to check the dowsing survey at the east end of the north aisle. A north–south trench revealed a feature pre-dating the present north wall of *c.* 1350, probably a pre-Norman outer north wall within it.

A fire, started in the chancel's organ bay on 7th March (Ash Wednesday) 1984, did extensive damage besides destroying the organ. The new organ, which was completed in 1988, was planned by Nicholas Thistlethwaite, designed by Henry Moss and built by Peter Collins. It occupies a new west gallery (1987) reviving a traditional post-Reformation site before the 19th-century introduction of robed choirs in chancels. Below are raked semi-circular choir stalls. The organ, of original design, has the now favoured and revived simple mechanical action, and three keyboards, with the

great organ and pedal organ in the main case, the swell organ behind it, and the choir organ in a small case at the front of the gallery. The pipes of hammered lead have a mellow appearance; the carving by Siegfried Pietszch was inspired by notable early 17th-century examples stylistically consistent with Bishop John Cosin's work at Durham Cathedral, Brancepeth and Auckland Castle, and with bracket motifs from Gabriel Krammer's pattern book circulated in 1610.

The gallery, designed to relate to the new north door screen, inspired by box pews at Ninekirk (1661), has a balustrade reminiscent of work at Rycote chapel, Oxfordshire, *c.* 1630. Concerts frequently take place here, continuing the church's fine musical tradition.

Adjacent to the wall south of the churchyard was a hermit's cell or anchorage; and the tomb of St John Wharton, an anchorite, became a pilgrim shrine before the Reformation.

On the steep bank below the tower is St Oswald's Well, a clear spring, which once had an elegant arcaded well-head and platform, destroyed by vandals.

A footpath leaves Church Street by the war memorial cross, passing between the tower and St Oswald's Well to a tree-shaded walk high above the river to Prebends' Bridge.

Church Street and South Road

Church Street leads past Anchorage Terrace, built in connection with George and Henry Salvin's new cotton factory. They brought machinery here from Castle Eden in 1796, when a river and canal scheme to establish Durham as an industrial centre was revived. It was burnt down in 1804 and never rebuilt. When Elvet Pit was sunk the houses became 'Pit Row', but after its late 19th-century closure were renamed Anchorage Terrace from the nearby anchorage site.

At the crossroads, Quarry Heads Lane turns right by a playing field opposite the New Inn. In the hedge stands the stump of Charley's Cross (formerly Peaseby's Cross) moved from the opposite side of the crossroads, and perhaps once a boundary or sanctuary cross.

Opposite is South Road. On the left corner are the University's science laboratories and the new University Library (1982). Beyond on the left are Grey College (1959) and Collingwood College (1971). On the right is Trevelyan College (1967) and a lane to Van Mildert College (1965) and St Aidan's College (1964), near Elvet Hill House, former home of the architect Ignatius Bonomi, and now the University's Oriental Department. The magnificent Museum of Oriental Art, added in 1959, is open to the public (*see page 29*).

Hallgarth Street

Returning to the crossroads, the road east joins Hallgarth Street at Mount Joy, overlooked by high ground. Tradition claims that the Community of St Cuthbert first saw the Durham peninsula from here when they arrived in 995 with the body of

St Cuthbert, to settle and build their great church. The road to the south (A177) leads through tree-shaded Shincliffe Peth past Houghall Agricultural College. Behind houses on the east side of Hallgarth Street stood the hostillar's hall or home farm. The fine half-timbered tithe barn and checker of 1446–7 are now a prison officers' club.

New Elvet

Hallgarth Street leads down to New Elvet. Beyond the junction with Church Street, Kingsgate Bridge on the left crosses the river as pedestrian access to the peninsula. Beside it, Dunelm House (student centre), and Elvet Riverside (University arts lecture rooms) are opposite Court Lane which follows the boundary between Elvet barony and the monks' borough of Elvet.

Below Court Lane, a large double-fronted 18th-century house is now the Durham City Police Headquarters. It was owned in the early 19th century by John Gregson, an attorney. During the 1930s, when the top front windows retained nursery safety bars, the ghost of a small girl, in a long skirt, cap, button boots and with her hands in a muff, sometimes appeared in a top landing doorway singing nursery rhymes. She has been associated with the name Anne Gregson scratched with a diamond above the date 1808 in a south end rear window. She has re-appeared recently.

Court Lane leads to the head of Old Elvet and New Elvet joins the foot of Old Elvet at Elvet Bridge.

Old Elvet

Facing pleasant gardens at the head of Old Elvet stand the combined Assize Courts, by Francis Sandys (1809–11) and Durham Prison, completed 1819 by Moneypenny and Ignatius Bonomi. St Cuthbert's church opposite, also by Bonomi (1827) symbolises Old Elvet's reputation as a refuge for Roman Catholics under persecution. Old Elvet was a

Elvet Bridge from Fearon's Path, rising towards the site of the former bridge tower. On the right is a formerly 'wet' arch of the original 12th-century bridge and the remains of St Andrew's Chapel (built 1274–83), now a shop (*see also page 11*). *Durham City Council.*

15th-century road south. Its broad street, graced by dignified Georgian façades, accommodated horse fairs until this century. Outside no. 21, one lamp standard remains of several erected in 1824 to contend with disorder. They burnt whale oil from Hull. The elegant balcony of no. 30 overlooks the site of Old Elvet's public well among trees. Lady Elizabeth Milbanke, relative of Byron's wife, once lived at no. 34, as later did J. B. Dykes. The Masonic Hall, a mock-gothic design by Ebdy (1869), the Old Shire Hall (1895–7), now University offices, and Elvet Methodist church with its spire (1903) break a former stylistic unity.

The Royal County Hotel was formerly two houses. The handsome staircase of 1680, from the demolished Stroughton Hall, near Leicester, was installed in the hotel in 1926. Lady Mary Radclyffe (a Derwentwater of Dilston) had occupied one house, maintaining there 'Mr Ferdinando Ashmole a Popish priest' whose burial was recorded at St Oswald's. Her half-sister was Lady Mary Tudor, natural daughter of Charles II; James, her nephew, was executed after the 1715 rebellion; and his brother Charles allegedly hid here before his arrest for treason after the '45. Elizabeth Bowes, aunt of Lord Strathmore's wife, Mary Eleanor Bowes, owned the house from 1758. On the hotel balcony, between 18th-century pilasters, leading politicians appear each third Saturday of July at the Durham Miners' Gala. Miners' Lodges follow banners and bands to the playing-fields (Smiddyhaughs – *smooth river meadows*), Durham's Race Course 1733–1887. Since the closing of the Durham pits, the Miners' Gala has lost much of its impetus and its future is uncertain. (*See also picture on page 11.*)

Through the archway was Chapel Passage, now demolished, named from a Wesleyan chapel opened there in 1808. (John Wesley, who died in 1791, probably preached in an earlier chapel, a converted house also vanished, in Court Lane.) Beyond is the elegant former Masonic Hall, begun in 1809. At the corner, the Waterloo, a former coaching inn, was destroyed in 1971 to give access to the new bridge.

Elvet Bridge (Elvet end)

From here, pedestrians should use the medieval bridge to reach the city centre. At the Elvet end of the bridge on the left, on a bridge pillar beside a formerly 'wet' arch, the remains of St Andrew's chapel, founded between 1274 and 1284 by William son of Absolam, are camouflaged by a Dutch-gabled building. After the dissolution of chantries it had various uses. In the 18th century it was used partly as a blacksmith's shop (and remained so until this century); while a charity school was taught in what appeared to have been the chancel. (*See also page 11.*)

THE BANKS

Steps lead from the foot of Silver Street to the riverside. The upper footpath mounts beside a crenellated garden wall built west of the earlier fortifications. From this path, Windy Gap branches up to Palace Green. The path leads past the former Broken Walls quarry, where Bishop Flambard's fortification wall fell. From here in 1663 stone was quarried for Castle restoration. The path continues below the Cathedral's west end to join the lower one near Prebends' Bridge. Between the upper and lower paths is St Cuthbert's Well, its well-head dated 1690, restored in 1987. It was provided after the Galilee Well's outer dip-well (*see page 7*), now visible only below a grating in the subsequently raised path, could no longer be used by the public.

Water was obtained from several springs in the Banks and wells sunk near to the Cathedral and Castle. In this region ground water collects in permeable sandstone near to the surface which overlies a thin coal seam and a layer of impermeable clay. Springs occur where the water escapes above the clay bands in the sides of the Banks, such as at St Cuthbert's Well and St Oswald's Well (*see page 20*). Wells sunk through the sandstone bands to the clay beneath provide a good water supply, like those in the College and some of the houses in the Bailey.

On the lower footpath, two corn mills were, from *c.* 1500, known as the Jesus Mills, as their profits financed the Cathedral's Jesus (nave) altar. Their buildings are now together the Old Fulling Mill, the University's Museum of Archaeology (*see also page 28–29*). One mill was leased for carding and fulling in 1792. The weir served also two mills opposite for corn and fulling.

The river is popular for boating and Durham School and individual colleges own boathouses.

Prebends' Bridge, designed by George Nicholson (1777), replaced a wooden footbridge of 1574, and a stone bridge of 1696, swept away except for abutments up-river, in the 1771 flood. The monks had a ferry to Crossgate Manor.

Close to Prebends' Bridge, thirteen elm trunks from trees which died of Dutch elm disease, have been set upright in an apparently random group, 14 ft by 17 ft by 22 ft. From them has been created a representation entitled the Upper Room, the scene of the last meal taken by Jesus with his disciples before his crucifixion. Twelve of the trunks are carved and the thirteenth is hollowed out as a seat seen from which they form into a room with round-headed windows, and a table set with utensils as though left from a meal: the Last Supper. The creator of this impressive scene is the sculptor, Colin Wilbourn of Sunderland, Artist-in-Residence in Durham Cathedral 1986–7 and the first local person to hold this annual appointment, living in St Chad's College and financed by the Dean and Chapter of Durham Cathedral and Northern Arts. During his residence he carved also the Kathedra, a large stone sculpture beneath Prebends' Bridge. Its name recalls that the word Cathedral is derived from the Latin *Cathedra*, the seat from which a bishop in early times taught his followers. Another sculpture from the same hand may be seen in the University Botanic Garden (*see page 29*).

The Upper Room: an imaginative group of carved elm trunks which resolve themselves into the scene of the Last Supper, when the visitor occupies the seat (representing Christ's place) at the end farthest away from Prebends' Bridge. *Durham City Council.*

On the west bank two rising paths lead, right, to South Street (one passes South Street well, a strong, clear spring); the road is to the White Gates and Quarry Heads Lane, named from the sacrists' quarry which supplied stone for the Cathedral. The left path follows the river to St Oswald's churchyard, or, by branching right beside a cascading stream, climbs to Church Street head. Bases of turrets among the trees mark former air shafts to Elvet Colliery whose pit-head is now the University science site.

Returning across Prebends' Bridge, the road leads to South Bailey. The footpath, right, continues beside the river past the mis-named 'Count's House' (*c.* 1820–30), a classical style garden house to 12, South Bailey. (*See also page 12 for Count Boruwlaski.*) Below, nearer the river, stood the cottage where the Miss Ebdons kept house for the 'Little Count'.

Nearby is the long course finishing post of England's oldest regatta, established in 1834 some years before Henley. The path continues, with the

Prebends' Bridge frames the old mill house at the west end of the weir below the Cathedral. *Claughton Photography.*

The Banks and South Street Mill: one of four which once relied on the weir below the Cathedral. *Margot Johnson.*

Peninsula walls high above, to pass beneath Kingsgate Bridge. Fearon's Path, connecting Bow Lane steps and Elvet Bridge, was paved by Dr Andrewes Fearon of Winchester, Durham School's headmaster 1882–4, to benefit town and University rowing enthusiasts.

Boats may be hired at Brown's boathouse, between Elvet Bridge and New Elvet Bridge, and paths follow the river past Baths Bridge, by the swimming baths, to continue in pleasant riverside walks.

UNIVERSITY OF DURHAM

History

This, the fourth oldest English University, began as a purely ecclesiastical foundation on 28th October 1833. It originated in the Cathedral Chapter Act of 1831, which led to the Durham University Bill of 1832. Under Archdeacon Thorp as Warden, 19 foundation scholars and 18 others took up residence in Archdeacon's Inn, Palace Green. A Royal Charter was granted in 1837.

The bishops' Castle, granted with church estates in 1839–40, provided the new **University College** with a hall larger and more beautiful than any at Oxford and incomparable buildings.

There had been earlier university schemes. From *c.* 1286 Durham Priory sent youths to Durham Hall, Oxford, which became an endowed College in 1380. As monastic property, Durham College surrendered to Henry VIII, who planned to re-found it with provost, 4 readers, 9 scholars, 10 divinity students at Oxford and 10 at Cambridge, schoolmaster and usher. Durham's new Dean and Chapter returned it to the King in 1544 and it passed in 1556 to Trinity College (founded 1555) with Durham connections severed.

After the Castle and Cathedral passed into secular hands under the Commonwealth, Parliament received three general local petitions (1649–52) inspired, perhaps, by an unsuccessful Elizabethan plan for a College at Ripon to serve the North. Following a fourth petition, presented personally to Oliver Cromwell in 1657, the mayor and aldermen

Hatfield College: occupies a unique position in the heart of the city, adjacent to the Cathedral and Castle, and above the wooded banks of the River Wear. During vacations it offers board and accommodation for tourists and visitors to Durham. (Tel: (0191) 374 3165. Fax: (0191) 374 7472.)

were instructed to 'set out so much of the Cathedral as shall be necessary for a chapel and schooles'. The College was to be financed by sequestered Cathedral funds and subscriptions. Letters Patent of 14th May, 1657, provided for a provost, 2 preachers or senior fellows, 12 fellows (i.e. 4 professors, 4 tutors and 4 schoolmasters – in the Oxford sense), with endowments for 24 scholars and 12 exhibitioners; while the 'free school' was attached under existing masters. University status, petitioned for immediately, was opposed successfully by Oxford and Cambridge. Cromwell died in 1658; and when the monarchy was restored in 1660, the Cathedral and its revenues reverted to the re-constituted Dean and Chapter. The infant college closed.

The scheme of 1831 has succeeded and the University, like its predecessors at Oxford and Cambridge, is collegiate. Its colleges and other buildings are scattered widely throughout the city and its outskirts.

In 1839, the University purchased astronomical instruments and a telescope. The architect Antony Salvin designed an **Observatory** which was built by public subscription in 1841 south-west of the Peninsula; and the Duke of Northumberland presented a refractory telescope in 1846. It was removed when the building was refurbished in the 1960s. An Obelisk erected on Western Hill by W. L. Wharton in 1850 marks the meridian 1,200 yards north. The Observatory holds the longest weather records in England, kept since 1847, for which it has been commended recently by the Meteorological Office.

Hatfield College, named after Bishop Thomas Hatfield (1345–81) was founded in 1846 in the old 'Red Lion' coaching inn and elegant assembly rooms of *c.* 1770 (*see page 10*) which remain, with the chapel of 1853, the nucleus of its present college buildings in the North Bailey. It is, therefore, one of the oldest provincial establishments in the country and at present accommodates undergraduate and post-graduate students, whose studies cover the entire spectrum of courses in the University.

Following the success of 'Hatfield', Archdeacon's Inn on Palace Green was revived in 1851 as Bishop Cosin's Hall, but had to be closed in 1864. It now serves as additional accommodation for University College.

The College of St Hild and St Bede: set in 16 acres of landscaped gardens off Gilesgate, it overlooks the river, Cathedral and Castle. Accommodation is available during vacations for conferences and individual families.

(Tel: (0191) 374 3079. Fax: (0191) 374 3064.)

Growth was slow, but Newcastle upon Tyne's **Durham College of Medicine** (1870) and **Durham College of Science** (1871) greatly increased student intake. The affiliated Codrington College, Barbados, and Fourah Bay College, Sierra Leone, also granted Durham degrees.

Intending teachers were admitted to **Bede College** for men (1841) with buildings 1845–7 and **St Hild's College** for women (1858), both Church of England Diocesan Training Colleges. These, united, became a member College of the University in 1979.

Unattached or non-collegiate students were first admitted to the University in 1871; and as numbers increased, they developed a corporate life for social and athletic activities. **St Cuthbert's Society**, founded in 1888, has been based in the South Bailey

St Cuthbert's Society: the main building, 12, South Bailey, with its adjacent properties. Accommodation enquiries to 12, South Bailey. (Tel: (0191) 374 3400. Fax: (0191) 374 4753.)   *John Norton.*

St Mary's College: the main building, designed in stone by Vincent Harris, has neo-classical proportions worthy of the view of the Cathedral, a gracious dining-room for receptions and a lovely chapel in the roof of the north-east wing. Visitors are welcome to stay in vacation time. (Tel: (0191) 374 2764. Fax: (0191) 374 7473.)

since 1951. It became a mixed society in 1969. Eighty of its 400 members – about a third of whom are mature students – live in South Bailey and the rest in other city properties.

Women were first admitted to degrees by the supplemental charter of 1895, obtained through the energy of Dean Waddington. Four St Hild's students enrolled immediately and 'Home' students followed.

A women's hostel opened in 1899 in Abbey House, Palace Green and became **St Mary's College** in 1919. It transferred to Elvet Hill in 1952.

St Chad's Hall, in the North Bailey, and **St John's** Hall in the South Bailey, were founded in 1904 and 1909 mainly, but not solely, for Anglican candidates for the ministry; and both are now Colleges. St John's added subsequently Cranmer Hall for their post-graduate training, to which women were admitted in 1966. St John's became open to women undergraduates from 1973 and St Chad's from 1988.

Essential local expansion off the Peninsula began in 1924 with the Dawson Building, South Road, containing the first botany, chemistry, geology and

St Chad's College: the smallest of the University colleges, has 175 undergraduates. It is ideal for use by small conferences and casual guests during vacations. Situated in the North Bailey opposite the east end of the Cathedral, the College is only 5 minutes' walk from the city centre, and yet enjoys a rare sense of peace and tranquillity. Any enquiries should be addressed to the Administrative Assistant. (Tel: (0191) 374 3370. Fax: (0191) 374 3360.)   *Arthur Pickett.*

St John's College: part of Cranmer Hall, which prepares candidates for the Christian ministry. This Church of England College for 250 students occupies former South Bailey residences, mostly 18th-century, close to the Cathedral. Accommodation, teaching facilities and equipment are available for conference groups (including non-Anglicans) during University vacations. Bed and breakfast enquiries welcome. (Tel: (0191) 374 3566. Fax: (0191) 374 3573.)

physics laboratories. The West buildings were added in 1950–1 with the Applebey Theatre, designed by J. S. Allen. Expansion on the Science Site has continued to the present day.

Grey College, founded in 1959, occupies the adjacent Fountains Field, from whose natural springs Durham Priory obtained piped water. The College is named after the 2nd Earl Grey who, as Prime Minister, signed the Bill founding Durham University. Its quadrangles and detached buildings are arranged to command the widest possible views of the city. The doors to its dining hall were presented and were once part of the annexe to Westminster Abbey built for the Queen's coronation.

Grey College: the main hall. The College stands in pleasant grounds close to woodland, and has a fine view to the Cathedral. Conferences and bed and breakfast visitors welcomed. (Tel: (0191) 374 2964. Fax: (0191) 374 2992.)

V. Watts.

A second body of women 'Home' students, using a variety of houses, became **St Aidan's** Society in 1947 and a College in 1961. In 1964 it moved to new buildings above St Mary's College and close to the Oriental Department and Museum. It now takes both men and women.

St Aidan's College: a delightful, modern, mixed University College designed by Sir Basil Spence, architect of Coventry Cathedral. Just 1 mile south of the city, it enjoys one of the finest views over the Cathedral. St Aidan's garden is open to the public and a guide book is available. During twenty-five weeks of University vacation, the College is used for holidays and conferences. (Tel: (0191) 374 3269. Fax: (0191) 374 4749.)

Van Mildert College, opened in 1966, is named after Bishop William Van Mildert, last of the prince-bishops and a founder of the University. Its pleasant site off South Road is enhanced by a lake with wild fowl and fish.

Trevelyan College followed in 1967 on the opposite corner of Mill Hill Lane in tranquil wooded surroundings. The unusual architecture was designed by John Eastwick-Field. Its name

Van Mildert College: located in a well-wooded park-like setting, adjoining a public golf course and opposite the Oriental Museum and Botanic Garden, and only 1 mile from the city centre. The buildings are attractively grouped around lawns and a small lake. Accommodation available throughout the year for holiday visitors on a daily or weekly basis; spacious lounge-bar and TV room; well-furnished single and twin-bedded rooms, all with wash-basins; newest building has luxury bedrooms with *en suite* facilities, TV, etc. For further information ring the Conference Administrator. (Tel: (0191) 374 3900. Fax: (0191) 374 3974.)

Trevelyan College: set in parkland within 1 mile of the city centre, this is one of the most exciting buildings in the North-East. It gained a Civic Trust Award in 1969 for its outstanding contribution to the surrounding scene. Excellent accommodation is offered during vacations for families and conferences. (Tel: (0191) 374 3764. Fax: (0191) 374 3789.)

Trevelyan College.

commemorates George Macaulay Trevelyan (of Wallington Hall, Northumberland), Regius Professor of Modern History at Cambridge University 1927–40, Master of Trinity College, Cambridge 1940–51 and Chancellor of Durham University 1950–58.

Collingwood College, founded in 1971, is named after Sir Edward Collingwood, Chairman of the University Council 1963–70. It has the distinction of being the first to be founded as a mixed College. The

first students entered in 1972. The monumental buildings, dominated internally by restful vistas of surrounding trees, lie near the site of Oswald House, whose wooded grounds the architect, Richard Sheppard of London, has used as an integral part of his scheme.

Collingwood College: Durham's newest college, situated in attractive woodland overlooking the Botanic Garden and only 1 mile from the city centre. The 213 *en suite* bedrooms coupled with unrivalled cuisine make Collingwood perfect for holiday makers and conferences alike. Bar, TV lounge, games room and tennis courts all on site; plenty of free car parking. English Tourist Board rating: 3 Crowns Commended. Welcome Host. Contact reception. (Tel: (0191) 374 4568. Fax: (0191) 374 4595.)

Teikyo University of Japan in Durham: established in April 1990, it gives Japanese undergraduate students the opportunity of spending one year studying in an English academic environment alongside the students of the University of Durham. The two Universities enjoy close academic, social, cultural and sporting links at all levels. Its Lafcadio Hearn Cultural Centre is available for private meetings or functions. Catering arrangements and overnight accommodation available on request. (Tel: (0191) 383 0733. Fax: (0191) 386 2584.)

Philip Nixon.

Kingsgate Bridge, designed by Ove Arup, was built jointly by the University and the city to connect the Peninsula with the new developments in Elvet to the east and south-east, where the latest building is the main **University Library**, begun in 1982 at the corner of South Road (*see also pages 5 and 20*). **Dunelm House**, at the eastern end of the footbridge, contains the Student and Staff Centre, which has facilities for visitors during vacations.

The Museum of Archaeology occupies the Old Fulling Mill on the riverside path below the Cathedral's western towers. From Palace Green, take the path through Windy Gap and descend the steps signposted to the Museum. There is no vehicular access. Disabled access possible from South Bailey, but to ground floor of Museum only. Open: April to October 11 a.m. to 4 p.m. daily; November to March, Wednesday to Sunday 12.30 p.m. to 3 p.m. (subject to alteration). Closed 24 and 25 December. Adults 80p, concessions 40p, children 20p. Groups welcome at group rate. (Tel: (0191) 374 3623.)

Claughton Photography.

Museum of Archaeology

The Museum of Archaeology occupies the Old Fulling Mill (formerly a corn mill) below the Cathedral's western towers and welcomes visitors (*see also page 22*). The Department of Archaeology has conducted numerous excavations on Roman and medieval sites, including those in the city and some of the discoveries are displayed here attractively.

Among them is material from the ruined medieval

manor house of the Prior of Durham at Bearpark (Beaurepaire), 2–3 miles west of the city. The site, which belongs to the City Council, is open to the public and has a picnic area (*see pages 36–37*).

Temporary displays are held in the newly refurbished upper gallery.

Oriental Museum

One of the less obvious treasures of Durham, the collection of Oriental Art, is housed in the Durham University Oriental Museum. It consists primarily of three major divisions, the Chinese ceramics collected by the Right Honourable Malcolm MacDonald who was Chancellor of the University from 1970 to 1981, the collection of Egyptian antiquities made by the 4th Duke of Northumberland in the 1820s and a vast group of Chinese jade and other hardstone carvings given to the University by Sir Charles Hardinge. These are supplemented by objects from other parts of the Orient and the result is regarded by connoisseurs all over the world as a major museum of Oriental Art.

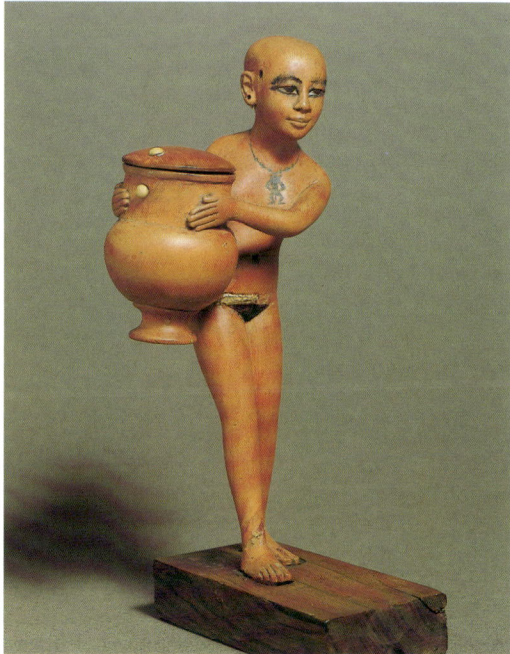

Oriental Museum: boxwood figure of a servant girl, from Egypt *c.* 1400 BC; she is 7 inches high, carries an amphora which once contained a cosmetic, and is notable for the unusual naturalistic pose. Museum open: weekdays 9.30 a.m.–1 p.m.; 2–5 p.m.; Saturday and Sunday 2–5 p.m. Closed Christmas to New Year. (Tel: (0191) 374 2911.)

Botanic Garden

The University of Durham Botanic Garden covers 18 acres among the woodland and countryside 1 mile south of Durham City. Mature trees shelter some of the more unusual plants collected from all over the world. Two small glass houses, one for rainforest plants and the other for cacti are popular with visitors.

The new Alpine Garden is made up of two raised beds and a limestone Rock Garden. The south aspect

creates a micro-climate which also provides a sheltered place for visitors to sit.

The Woodland and Primula Gardens are best seen in spring while the rose pergola is a summer feature. Heathers and rich autumn colours on the North American trees are spectacular at other times. The award winning Prince Bishops' Garden, designed and sponsored by Durham County Council for the Gateshead Garden Festival, was relocated at the Botanic Garden in the summer of 1991. The theme of the figures by Colin Wilbourn is *In the Shadow of the Past*. Treated trunks of trees, which had died from Dutch elm disease, were used from Houghall Agricultural College, Durham, and from Wolsingham, Weardale. Each figure is shadowed by steel fretwork which, if viewed from a central seating area, becomes a relevant scene. The first group represents: 1. William of St Calais (Carilef), bishop 1081–96, responsible for Durham Cathedral's chancel and choir aisles: the shadow shows the Cathedral today. 2. Ralph, Lord Neville of Raby (d. 1367), commander at the victory of Neville's Cross in 1346: the shadow is Raby Castle. 3. John Cosin, bishop 1660–72, restorer after the Civil War and Commonwealth: the shadow depicts his chapel at Auckland Castle. The second group relates to the industrial era: 1. A member of the Shafto family, leading county colliery owners: the shadow illustrates the pit-head and winding gear at Seaham. 2. George Stephenson, 1781–1848, pioneer of railways: his shadow is the railway viaduct, Chester-le-Street. 3. Sir James Laing, b. 1823, representing ship-building on the Wear: shadowed by Sunderland shipyards.

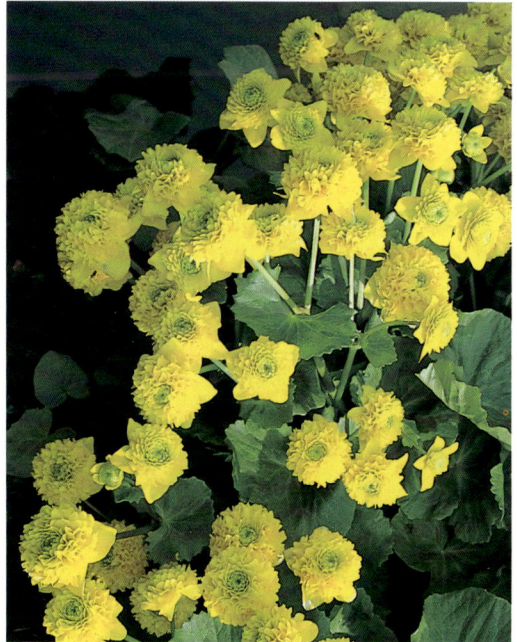

The University Botanic Garden: Caltha pallustris 'Flora Plena'. The Garden is open every day of the year. The glass houses are open daily, 9.00 a.m. to 4 p.m. The Visitors' Centre with cafeteria is open 10 a.m. to 5 p.m. every day March to October inclusive and 1.00 p.m. to 3.30 p.m. November to February (weather permitting) but closed Christmas week. *Mike Hughes.*

PLACES TO VISIT IN THE NEIGHBOURHOOD

OLD DURHAM AND OLD DURHAM GARDENS

Old Durham, 1 mile east of the city, is reached either by a riverside path (15 minutes' walk), or by a lane leading south from Sherburn Road. River trips are planned to Strawberry Landing beside the wild flower meadow below the gardens. (For Maiden Castle, Roman and Dark Age remains *see inside front cover.*)

Early History

A road formerly ran from the south through Old Durham, crossing higher ground to the north before dropping to a ford at Kepier. In 1782 John Cade, the antiquary, conjectured it was Roman. The name Old Durham occurs in the earliest local documents, suggesting an ancient settlement.

By the 12th century William, rector of St Nicholas, held the manor of Old Durham where a later rector, Galfrid de Helme, obtained permission for an oratory in his 'court' in 1268. Rectors held manorial courts at Old Durham for their tenants. Their house possibly suffered before 1330 when the Scots burnt Sherburn Hospital.

The River Wear changed its course forming, in the 15th century, a partly dried up ox-bow lake north of Maiden Castle. Both old and new river beds appear on a plan made *c.* 1440–50 when questions arose about Durham Priory's liability to maintain a road tending to flood near Scaltok Mill at Old Durham.

In 1443, Bishop Robert Neville impropriated the rectory of St Nicholas to Kepier Hospital, which afterwards appointed a stipendiary curate to the church, while the income from Old Durham manor augmented the revenues of the hospital (*see page 18*).

In 1474, Robert Booth, Master of Kepier, leased the manor to his brother, Richard, for 99 years (reserving the timber of Pelaw Wood and £10 rent).

River Wear near Old Durham Gardens: Maiden Castle on right. *Margot Johnson.*

When religious houses were dissolved in 1546, the Crown confiscated Kepier Hospital property. After passing through several hands, John Heath, a wealthy Protestant merchant, Warden of the Fleet Prison (and sometime of Kings Lynn), acquired it in 1569. Probably the only purchaser of former northern religious property to do so, he resided in the old hospital. Noted for his generosity, he doubled the

Old Durham Gardens: view across the Wear Valley to Durham Cathedral and Castle from the upper garden wall and gazebo. *R. MacBride.*

endowment of Kepier Grammar School at Houghton-le-Spring, and was granted arms (*party per chevron, or and sable, in chief two mullets, in base a heathcock, counterchanged*).

His purchase was subject to the lease of Old Durham. When a later Robert Booth died in 1592, he left by will the house and other property to his wife and children under age. The inventory lists a hall, many chambers, chapel chamber, and chambers in the curtain wall, and seems typical of medieval houses with stabling and men-at-arms quarters above, in its courtyard. Robert had bought recently a house in Old Elvet.

John Heath died in 1591. An oak recumbent effigy in St Giles' chancel represents him in Elizabethan plate armour, head resting on a tilting helmet with the Heath cock crest.

His son John Heath II succeeded him, built Kepier House, and died there in 1618, leaving as heir his eldest son John III, then 49, the last at Kepier, whose only child Thomas died in infancy in 1594.

The title to Kepier property was vested in his brother Thomas Heath of Kepier West Grange whose son, John Heath IV (1604–65) when barely 19, married Margaret, daughter of William Smith of Durham, in 1623. In December 1630, Thomas and John IV sold the house, gardens and orchards of Kepier to Ralph Cole of Gateshead, whose son and grandson, Sir Nicholas and Sir Ralph Cole, resided there until 1674, although John Heath III lived there until his death in January 1640.

The Heaths and Tempests

Old Durham was settled on John IV and Margaret in 1630, but they lived in North Bailey. Their only child Elizabeth was baptised in October 1626 at St Mary-le-Bow, where John IV was churchwarden and in 1637 gave land for its churchyard. In February 1642 he was still a parishioner, described as 'Counsellor at lawe', and on 27th October that year Elizabeth married there John Tempest of the Isle (near Sedgefield), son of Sir Thomas Tempest, Attorney-General of Ireland.

John Heath IV was living at Old Durham in 1652, dying there in 1665 when John Tempest and Elizabeth succeeded him.

John Tempest I of Old Durham, described in a political pamphlet of 1677 as 'a papist, a pensioner, and a court-dinner man', became a strong supporter of the exiled James II. Their eldest daughter, Margaret, married Sir Richard Shuttleworth of Forcett (south of Gainford) and when Elizabeth died in October 1684 and John I in July 1697 (both buried at Forcett), William, their eldest surviving son, inherited Old Durham. William had married in 1677 (at Forcett), Elizabeth, daughter of John Sudbury, Dean of Durham, and was M.P. for Durham City in 1678, 1680 and 1689. In 1699 he was known as Colonel Tempest; he died in March 1700 and was buried at St Giles.

His son and heir, John Tempest II (1679–1737), became M.P. for the County in 1705 and in the following year married the heiress Jane Wharton; but by 1719 they had left Old Durham for Sherburn while John's mother, Elizabeth, lived in Old Elvet where she died in June 1728. John died in 1737, a few months after his wife, and their son John Tempest III (1710–76) inherited the estates. He married Frances Shuttleworth of Forcett, at Merrington, in May 1738 and was M.P. for the City of Durham 1741–61. He bought Wynyard in 1742 but was living at Sherburn when he made his will in 1771. At Old Durham he employed a gardener, James, to maintain the gardens. John Tempest III was buried at St Giles on 17th May 1776.

Old Durham Gardens: the steps below the gazebo. From 1997, the upper garden opens to visitors from Easter to September, with the gazebo furnished in 17th-century style. On the lower floor an exhibition is planned to tell the story of the site. *Durham City Council.*

His son and heir, John Tempest IV, of Wynyard (and Brancepeth Castle) married Anne Townshend, and was M.P. for Durham between 1768 and 1790. An estate plan drawn up for him in September 1776 shows there were two upper walled gardens, with a path alongside their joint long western wall, the gardens below this sloping towards the Beck, a formal garden with geometrically laid out walks north of the mansion site adjacent to Pelaw Woods, and a bridle road leading from Durham across a ford and skirting the western side of the gardens to join the present lane at Old Durham Farm.

Old Durham Gardens: flights of stone steps, nine feet wide, descend from the gazebo and connect the terraces.
Claughton Photography.

An account of the 1780s describes the gardens:

Old Durham house is gone to decay, nothing now remaining but apartments for a farmer ... The gardens are formed into terraces of considerable length. This sweet retirement is become a place for public resort, where concerts of sweet music have been frequently performed in the summer, and the company regaled with fruit, tea, etc. The gardens are open all summer for rural recreation. At the corner of the garden some few years ago were the remains of a very ancient building, with a circular window, and other appearances of the chapel form.

Excavations here in the 1960s revealed stone walls with medieval hard plaster on the interior.

The only child of John Tempest IV was John Wharton Tempest who died unmarried aged 21 at Brighton in 1793. John IV died in 1794, and was buried at St Giles. The entire inheritance now passed to the descendants of his sister Frances, who had married, at St Mary-le-Bow in 1768, the Reverend Sir Henry Vane, LL.D. (1771–1813), Rector of Long Newton and a Canon of Durham Cathedral.

Their son Sir Henry Vane (1771–1813) assumed the additional name of Tempest on inheriting the Tempest estates in accordance with his uncle's will.

The 19th Century

A plan of 1812 shows Old Durham divided into farms. Other details are omitted, but the gardens and adjoining house were let to 'Jos. Robinson'. Sir Henry Vane-Tempest's wife was Anne, Countess of Antrim and their daughter, Frances Anne Emily Vane-Tempest (1800–65) married Charles William Stewart (1778–1854), 3rd Marquess of Londonderry (see page 12).

By 1827 the Pineapple Inn stood on part of the site and remained a public house until the licence was lost in 1926 owing to its then unfavourable reputation. The historian, Robert Surtees, who died in 1834, wrote:

The house of Old Durham, the deserted seat of the Heaths and Tempests, stands warm and sheltered ... The main body of the house has been taken down; the gardens only remain formed into sloping banks and long terraces. An old summerhouse, with a small bay-window, has the initials J[ohn] H[eath].

In 1849 the Londonderrys sank the Lord Ernest Pit to the Hutton Seam and production continued until the end of the 19th century.

The first O.S. map of 1857 shows the north formal garden replanted as an orchard; the south walled garden was a bowling green, with the gazebo (its first firm appearance on a plan or map) at the west end of a raised terrace.

A 1924 *Guide to Durham* advertises Old Durham Gardens: 'Dancing, putting green, running track, tennis courts, ices, tea gardens and full licensed free house. Parties catered for'. A photograph taken from the back of the Pineapple shows four statues, one in a central flower bed. Older residents remember the running track below the slope of the lower garden with a small building for equipment against the stone wall at the north end.

Recent History

In 1893 the North Eastern Railway Company opened a station at Elvet. Branching off the line at Sherburn, this line crossed the Old Durham Estate and ran across the south-west corner of the lower garden on an embankment (still remaining). At the end of its life in the mid-1950s, it was used solely for carrying passengers to and from the annual miners gala.

In 1918 the 7th Marquess of Londonderry sold the Old Durham Estate in three lots chiefly to their former tenants, the Hopps family who still farm most of it today.

Part of the gardens was sold to St Hild's College in the 1930s for a proposed extension, never achieved, and sold to the City Council in 1985 when Richard Hopps sold the adjacent land to enable restoration.

Recent archaeological work has revealed a series of flights of steps *c.* 9 ft wide descending from the gazebo. The wall to its north is ancient; at its north end (in a private garden) are the remains of what may have been a garderobe, and blocked mullioned windows occur in various places in neighbouring walls, all on private property. Built into the wall to the east of the Pineapple is a door pediment and much weathered coat of arms. The adjacent farm buildings are 17th–18th-century.

PITTINGTON

The Community of St Cuthbert owned the ancient settlements of Pittington, which Bishop William of St Calais (1083–93) granted to their successors, the Durham Benedictines. From the Prior's Hall at Pittington Hall Garth, adjacent to the church, and rebuilt several times, they farmed the estate. Prior Hugh de Darlington built here a timber-framed camera (residence) in 1258, with accommodation for monks, resident bailiff, stables, dairy, kitchen, and other offices. Prior William de Ebchester demolished the hall in 1450, replacing it in stone, with ornate plasterwork and costly hangings. Manorial courts met here and priors made it a summer residence. Hugh Whitehead, the last prior (1524–40), rebuilt the complex within its walled courtyard.

At the dissolution of Durham Priory this, with the estate, was assigned to the 10th Prebendal Stall and leased. After 1580, the lessee built a new house, buying stone from the demolished priors' camera. The remains were removed in building a new 19th-century vicarage.

St Laurence's Church

The dedication suggests early origins. St Wilfred brought *brandeis* (cloth strips which had touched the Saint's bones) from the Pope to the King of Northumbria in A.D. 667. Laurence, a Roman deacon, refused to surrender church treasures during Valerian's persecution, producing instead the poor and sick in his care as his 'treasures'. The west window depicts his martyrdom by burning in A.D. 258.

The 10th–11th-century sundial (lacking a gnomon) on the exterior south wall is from the pre-Conquest church. Its five lines divided daylight hours into six. The mid-day line has a cross-bar and is flanked by two on each side with dots at two-thirds of their lengths. The five lines end in squares reminiscent of primitive systems with stones around a central post in the ground.

The plain sandstone font-bowl under the tower is just pre-Conquest. Replaced in 1808 by a pewter basin on a wooden pillar, it was sold in 1809 for a cattle trough, but restored in 1885.

In 1847, the Dean and Chapter offered Pittington the Cathedral's shell font of 1663 erected by Bishop John Cosin. Realising the mistake, its return was requested in 1935, and effected after some opposition from the parish. A richly carved oak cover of tabernacle work cost five shillings in 1628, and formerly hung over the font. The church was broken into recently and the font cover was stolen.

The Saxon church, with its small square chancel and high, aisleless nave twice the chancel's size, had small, deeply splayed windows, still visible above the later arcading. Two, above the north aisle's west end, contain 12th-century paintings in true fresco by the painter (or his associate) of the figures and draperies behind the Cathedral Galilee's north altar. Survivors of a series depicting St Cuthbert's life, one shows his consecration by Archbishop Theodore, with six other bishops and Ecgfrith, King of Northumbria, looking over his shoulder. The other illustrates Bishop Cuthbert's vision, during a meal with Abbess Aelfleda

Pittington, St Laurence: the west tower.   *R. H. Langdon.*

at Osingadun, of a Whitby brother's death in falling from a tree, and his soul being carried to heaven. Only central yellow lines remain of the tree; its branches and leaves have faded. Many other paintings survived until destroyed in 19th-century 'restoration'. These were covered by a west gallery. On its removal the enlightened vicar, Dr Miller (1822–54), rescued them from damage by workmen.

The nave's north arcade, of highly enriched transitional work, c. 1170, pierces the pre-Conquest north wall. Its arches, with chevron moulding on the inner side, supported by alternate pillars of spiral and fluted design developed from Durham Cathedral patterns, resemble and pre-date those of its Galilee, built in 1174–5 by Richard de Wolveston, called 'the Engineer', holder of land in Pittington and Newton, who died c. 1182. The Pittington arcade seems to be his, and as a devotee of St Cuthbert, he probably commissioned the frescos. As chief architect to Hugh of Le Puiset (Bishop of Durham 1154–95), he built also in 1170 the west part of Norham Keep, probably the Constable's Hall at Durham Castle, with its magnificent doorway, and, between 1170–74, Bowes Castle Keep for Henry II.

His successors as the Bishop's architects were William the engineer, and Christian the mason who held lands in South Sherburn and is buried here. His grave cover of Frosterley or Stanhope marble, wider at the top than the bottom, was rescued from the churchyard and now lies at the east end of the south aisle. The two-line Latin inscription means:

One bearing the name of Christ is buried in this grave.

Let him who beholds the grave commend him with a prayer to Christ.

An original, smaller, tower was contemporary with the north arcade. The present tower arch on pointed boutells indicates the earliest Early English period for its enlargement with the pointed windows the second stage, and the north semi-octagonal stair turret. The top stage with embattled parapet is Perpendicular work. The west window of 1585 contains later glass depicting the martyrdom of St Laurence on a gridiron. The tower was buttressed on the south wall in 1609. In the belfry, three medieval bells in an oak bell-frame (probably original) are inscribed:

+*Sca maria ora pro nobis* (St Mary pray for us);

+*Sca trinita vnvs devs miserere nobis* (Holy Trinity one God pity us);

+*Sancta marineta* (perhaps meant for St Margaret: a bad cast with other letters and traces of a date).

The first two bear the bell-founder's mark: three bells in a shield (Richard Pette?).

Further additions before 1250

The north arcade left an eastern respond (half pier) anticipating an extension: a chantry chapel outside the chancel's north wall with responds for a future open arch there, and opened to the north aisle by removing its east wall. A new long chancel was added east of the Saxon one, which now became part of the nave with its north wall replaced by the completed Early English arch to the chantry.

Next, the south doorway was widened. Its round arch was moved later in building the south aisle, and again at its rebuilding. It is still used.

The south aisle followed in about 1220, matching the lengthened north aisle but with pointed arches,

Pittington, St Laurence: a 12th-century arcade pierces the pre-Conquest north wall, creating an aisle for chantry chapels. The original high windows now look into the aisle, their wide splays embellished with important 12th-century paintings of scenes from the life of St Cuthbert. The later clerestory increases light in the nave. Open: 1 May to 30 September, Saturdays 2-4 p.m.; at other times by applying to 4 Prior's Grange, Pittington, Durham DH6 1DA. (Tel: (0191) 372 1773.) *G. Dresser.*

and the former Saxon chancel's wall was taken down. On the north side, the fifth arch was replaced (but leaving responds and capitals) by another to match the south arcade. At the south aisle's east end stood St Katherine's altar, for which Symon de Hawthorne and his wife Matilda left land to support a chantry priest.

Another chantry, St Mary the Virgin, was added later outside the new chancel's north wall and opening from it through two arches. Their pillars and responds had octagonal capitals enriched with foliage *en crochet*, similar to work in the Cathedral's Nine Altars (planned by Bishop Poore who died in 1237, and completed soon after 1278) and probably from the same source. This, and St Katherine's chantry had the same priest from 1419. When chantries were dissolved in 1547 it became a vestry; in 1624 a fireplace was inserted; and by 1784 it was demolished and its arches walled up. Later the remains of the carved foliage were reused in the north aisle.

The 19th century

An 1816 engraving depicts a north door with a square frame and late medieval pointed doorhead. Two steps descend into the north aisle, then paved to cover the pillar bases, suggesting much-risen outer and inner ground levels. A plan of 1835 shows a large west gallery (the population had risen with local coal mining), a vestry below in the north-west corner, and the font in the central aisle at its west end. The chancel, with the two former north chantry arches walled up, and a south priest's door, contained 'open sittings', a survival of the post-Reformation moving of communicants here from the nave at the Prayer of Humble Access; the three east lancet windows remained, but two early round-headed south windows had been blocked *c.* 1807 and one of churchwarden's Gothic substituted. All the nave windows had similar replacements.

Ignatius Bonomi designed alterations in 1846–7. The 12th-century chancel and chancel arch were demolished and rebuilt to lengthen the nave by adding another eastern bay on each side. To do this, both north and south 12th-century responds were moved a bay further east; the 13th-century arch from the north side was added to the south side which it matched and on the north side two new round arches were built with a new central pillar. The clerestory was new also.

The south aisle was rebuilt from its foundations, the 14th-century porch rebuilt, and its Norman doorway renovated. The north aisle was partially reconstructed, three Norman-style windows replacing two pointed ones and the doorway, with two more further east, one imitating 13th-century style; and at the east end, Bonomi reused the crocket capitals from the demolished north chapel. Outside, two surviving vertical slit windows about 4 inches wide and with deep inner splays just above ground level, were blocked and made invisible inside. The ground level has risen and their position relates to a formerly lower nave floor.

North of the chancel a new vestry with a north outer door was added, with an organ bay on its west side.

Later additions

The chancel screen of 1893 is by W. S. Hicks who designed lengthened aisles in 1897–8. In 1905 the now short chancel was extended eastward, heightened, and furnished (also by Hicks) with the intention to imitate late medieval arrangements. Robed choirs in parish churches became fashionable in the 19th century, copying cathedrals, hence a new organ, carved oak stalls for clergy and choir with panelling and bosses, sedilia against the sanctuary wall, an ancient credence table (perhaps from a former chantry) built into the south side, and elaborate pinnacled reredos with carved figures. The Lord's Prayer and Commandments were added.

Once removed to the churchyard from a former chantry, the recumbent effigy of *c.* 1280 in the north aisle is a knight in coat of mail and surcoat. His bassinet has the visor down with a horizontal slit for sight. His right hand holds an unsheathed cross-hilted sword with its raised blade partly covered by the shield in his left hand. Right of his crossed legs lies a small dog, and his mailed feet rest on an animal (a dragon?). The shield's armorial bearings are badly weathered, but were a fesse between three popinjays, arms of the Fitz Marmadukes, Lords of Horden in the adjacent Easington parish, and used also by the Lumleys and Thwengs.

Beside the font, an early 13th-century coped grave cover about 12 inches long has two toy swords for nobly-born infant twins. Nearby are other children's grave covers, one ornamental with a dentelle border and a galaxy of stars at the foot, besides fragments of Norman corbels and carved stones.

KELLOE AND COXHOE

For Kelloe, about 5 miles south-east of Durham, take A177. At Coxhoe traffic lights, turn left into B6291. In about ½ mile bear right for Kelloe. A drive, right, leads to Coxhoe Hall site (picnic area). Pass through Kelloe for the church, on low ground, right, by the beck.

Twenty-six of the seventy-four men killed in Trimdon Grange Colliery on 16th February 1888 lie buried beside their memorial in the extension churchyard.

St Helen's Church

St Helen's Norman tower, of three stages, has single belfry lights and two 12th- and 13th-century sweet-toned bells still in use. One is inscribed *Nomen meum Johannes est* (My name is John).

Enter by the south porch and early Norman doorway. The Norman north door is blocked. North and south blocked round-headed windows, visible externally, lit a former west gallery. The Norman nave has windows in later Perpendicular style; the Early English chancel has original lancets, with east and south Decorated period windows.

The north bay was St Mary's chapel or Pity Porch (from Our Lady of Pity – Mary at the cross when Jesus' body was removed) entered through a pointed arch and half a round one until the 18th century. In 1347, John Fitz Henry de Kellaw and his sister Elizabeth provided Morden lands for two chantry priests and Thornley lands for a third: hence its other

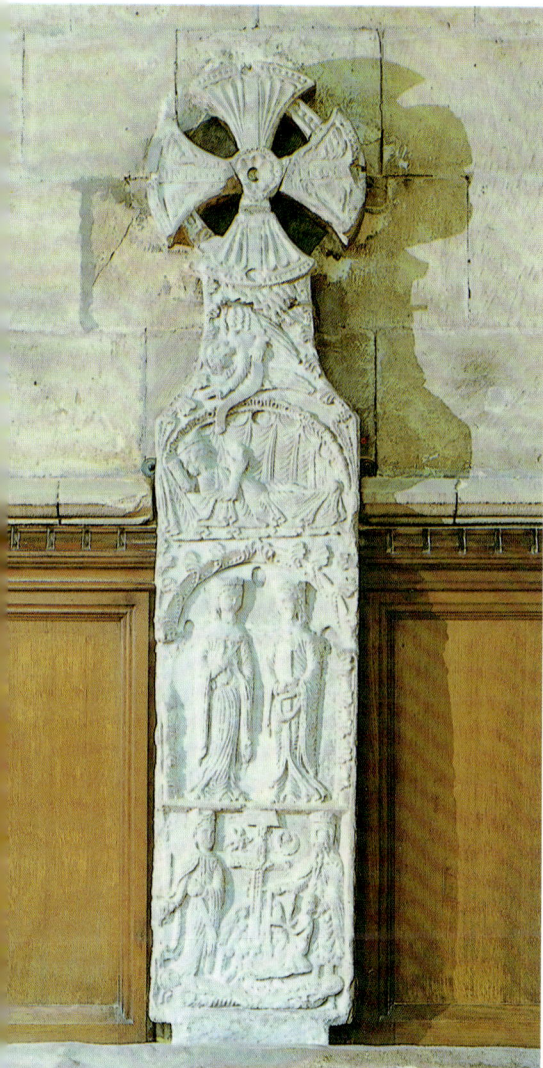

finding the 'True Cross'. This object of devotion on the pilgrim road to Durham is the most outstanding of its period in the north. It has affinities with early 12th-century sculpture in France, but its standing figures wear robes with folds in late 12th-century style, so dating the cross. During restorations in 1854 it was found, built into the chancel wall in two parts, lacking only part of the nimbus. In the top panel on the shaft, an angel with a scroll (originally lettered) points the reclining Emperor Constantine to the wheel crosshead inscription: IN HOC VINCES (*In this conquer*); the second portrays Constantine holding a cross, and St Helen, his wife, carrying a reliquary; third, Helen (with drawn sword) shows Judas the Jew (with spade) where to dig. They uncover two swathed corpses with crosses (? the thieves crucified with Christ). One, revived by Christ's cross, confirms its identity, raising a right hand in blessing.

The medieval tomb-lid nearby bears a foliated cross. On the nave's south side, a modern window depicts the Good Samaritan.

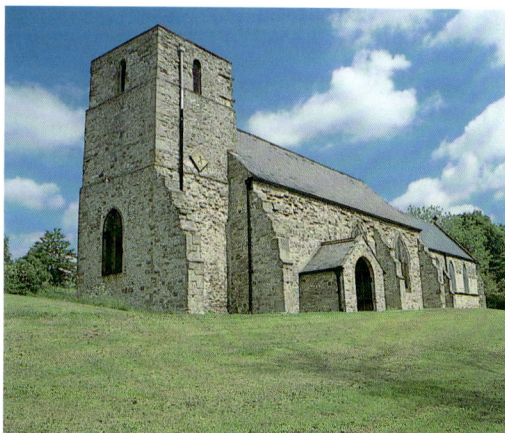

Kelloe, St Helen: the west tower and south porch. Church open to visitors: May to September, 2 to 4 p.m. Phone for other times and party visits. (Tel: (0191) 377 1053.)

Claughton Photography.

Kelloe, St Helen: the exquisite early 12th-century cross, probably sculpted in France, and once brilliantly coloured and gilded, stands against the sanctuary's north wall. Nine cavities may have held jewels or crystal-covered relics, one central in the cross-head being wood from the 'true cross'. Three panels depict: Constantine's dream; Helen, with book or reliquary, beside Constantine carrying a cross; and Helen (sword in hand) with Judas the Jew (holding spade) finding three crosses. The true one is revealed when its touch revives one of the corpses buried nearby. *T. Watson.*

name, the Thornley Porch. In the 19th century, it became a pew with a ceiling.

Joan, the last of the Kellaws, married John Fossour. Fossours lived here until the 17th century, moving to Harbourhouse, granted them by Richard Kellaw, bishop of Durham 1311–16. Their last heir, Basil Fossour, married Anne Tempest, and died without issue. John Tempest bought Kelloe. It passed to his nephew, Sir Henry Vane-Tempest and on his death in 1813, to Lady Frances Vane.

Against the sanctuary's north wall stands a beautiful Norman cross of fine greenish-grey sandstone, once brightly painted, depicting Helen

Elizabeth Barrett Browning

On the south wall, a marble slab is inscribed:

To commemorate the birth in this parish of Elizabeth Barrett Browning, who was born at Coxhoe Hall, 6th March, 1806, and died at Florence, 29th July 1861. A great poetess, a noble woman, a devoted wife. Erected by public subscription, 1897.

Kelloe remembers her annually on the date of her death, actually in June, not July!

The Burdons, earlier of Coxhoe Hall, built a gallery (since removed) across the tower arch in 1758; above it now hangs Charles II's handsome coat of arms, *c.* 1680. Below, in the 18th-century shell font, originally painted red, Elizabeth and her brother Edward (born 26th June 1807) were both baptised on 10th February 1808. The parish register records her as the 'first child and daughter of Edward Barrett Moulton Barrett of Coxhoe Hall, Native of St James, Jamaica, by his wife Mary, late Clarke, Native of Newcastle-upon-Tyne'.

Coxhoe Hall and the Moulton Barretts

In 1794 Charles Moulton, Elizabeth's grandfather, leased Coxhoe Hall. Here his wife brought their four children from Jamaica, after visiting John Graham-Clarke of Kenton Lodge, Newcastle-upon-Tyne, owner of estates in England and Jamaica, a coal mine, flax mills and a brewery. Edward Moulton, at 19, married Mary, first child of Graham-Clarke's second marriage, taking his bride home to Coxhoe Hall. Their first three children were born there before they left for Herefordshire in 1809.

In 1798, Edward and his brother Samuel inherited the estates of their maternal grandfather, Edward Barrett, adding the surname Barrett to their own. Edward believed his family cursed because its massive wealth derived from slave labour, a view his daughter shared. From this developed his excessively possessive attitude to his family, especially Elizabeth.

Coxhoe Hall, facing south across a landscaped park, and built in 1725 on the site of a 13th-century manor house, contained exceptionally fine plaster-work, probably by the Italian, Joseph Cortese. It passed in 1817 to Anthony Wilkinson, and in 1850 to Thomas Wood, whose descendants sold the estate to East Hetton Colliery Company (probably for underlying coal). The house stood empty until 1939 when it was commandeered for army use and later for Italian prisoners. Afterwards, squatters took over and vandalism followed. In 1947, it passed to the National Coal Board which declared it unsafe through mining subsidence, demolishing it in August 1952. In 1983, Durham City Council bought the site, which is now being landscaped for public access.

LUDWORTH TOWER

Take B1283 through Sherburn and at the top of Sherburn Hill turn right for Shadforth. One mile beyond the village, the ruin of Ludworth Tower rises on the left, with a picnic area.

Ludworth, originally the property of the de Ludworth family, passed in 1411 to the Holden family who built the present tower as the south-west part of an extensive manor house, now vanished. Bishop Langley granted Thomas Holden licence to crenellate and fortify it in 1422. Originally, outside steps led to the first floor entrance to the hall, from which the vaulted basement (probably used for secure storage) had its only access. A large part of the tower fell in 1890 and all that remains is part of the basement and, above, the west wall. It stands to a height of three storeys, with fireplaces on two, window openings, the remains of a garderobe and traces of a newel stair in the north-west corner. The present (Inclosure) road cuts across the site on the south where it slopes steeply to Shadforth Beck. The medieval village was deserted about 1450.

BEAUREPAIRE

For Beaurepaire, leave Durham by A690. At Neville's Cross traffic lights, turn right on to A167. At the Pot and Glass, turn left down Toll House Road for Bearpark, where take first turn right (signposted Bearpark Colliery). In ¼ mile, turn sharp right by former chapel (organ builder), following road where it bends left to colliery tip. In 200 yards, leave made road and turn right down unmade track. Continue for ½ mile, following colliery tip on right. After many bends, track drops into River Browney valley and Beaurepaire can be seen, right, on the hill side. Park on the flat ground at junction of track and old railway line.

Beaurepaire, favourite residence of Durham's medieval priors, lay central to a large park. Durham Priory acquired its nucleus c. 1195, made additions 1242–67, and emparked it by a ditch and bank with a timber fence. The park, at first used for cattle, included a 400 acre wood, and was further extended. After Bishop Antony Bek (1283–1310) broke down the fences and drove out the game during a dispute with Prior Hoton, stone walls replaced first the northern fences and later those elsewhere.

When Prior Bertram de Middleton resigned in 1258, Beaurepaire and other property was granted

Ludworth Tower: stands on a grassy knoll, now a picnic area, near the road which crosses the end of the formerly enclosed site of this once extensive residence of the Holden family.   *Durham City Council.*

Beaurepaire: at Bearpark, is 2–3 miles west of Durham. Finds from the excavations can be seen in the University's Museum of Archaeology (*see pages 28–29*).

Claughton Photography.

for his maintenance. He built here a camera (residence) with a chapel, used by later priors as a country retreat. Its estate, with barns and granaries, developed as a stud farm. The Durham monks had annual summer entertainment here, walking out across the fields with picnic tin plates and mugs.

Edward I was received here in 1296. The Scots, under Robert Brus devastated the county in 1315, surrounded the park, looted the chapel, carried off furnishings in the prior's cart and drove away 60 horses and 120 cows besides young cattle. The prior and monks escaped with difficulty.

Edward II was here in 1318; and Edward III in 1327, 1333 and 1335.

Before the Battle of Neville's Cross on 16th October 1346, King David (Brus) of Scotland's army camped in the park, doing much damage. Afterwards, Prior Fossour did extensive repairs besides making additions.

An inventory of 1464 lists a chapel, outer and inner chambers, hall, buttery and kitchen.

Hugh Whitehead, last Prior and first Dean of Durham, repaired and refurbished Beaurepaire, using it frequently and probably adding a gateway and the great south dormitory window. Until the Civil War, later deans used it occasionally, the last being Dean Hunt (1620–38), when there was only a large useless hall, a dining-room, and three or four other small rooms. In 1640, Scottish rebels destroyed part of the buildings and in 1644, 'quite destroyed them'.

Dean Granville's 1684 survey lists both contemporary and former apartments and gardens: 'a hall, two passages near the hall, one large kitchen and ovens in it, a back room adjoining on the west end of the kitchen, a dining-room, a great room leading to the chapel called the dormitory, some arches and two rooms above the arches, a chapel and a room under it, three rooms, or two at least called the prior's chamber, and the western room thereof called the prior's lodgings, a little room adjoining the prior's chamber, a staircase and vaults under all and every the lower or floor rooms of the said mansion house, excepting the hall and kitchen and the room aforesaid adjoining the kitchen. And at Beaurepaire aforesaid, there formerly have been belonging to the said manor house several courts and gardens that were walled about, and also sundry outhouses now wholly dilapidated'.

By 1787, only the chapel at the south end, a long east–west building at the north, and a long north–south building connecting them, remained. The rest was 'ruinous and confused'. In 1820 only the chapel and the adjoining gable still stood; but by 1846 the chapel was also a ruin.

Further collapses of stonework continued until, in 1979, the City of Durham accepted guardianship to save and consolidate what remained. Emergency work began in March 1980. Archaeologists working under Durham University Excavations Committee followed.

Excavations revealed the lower part of the dormitory's tall south gable and its undercroft, with windows having original 13th-century filletted roll moulding and 16th-century narrowing. The jamb of an upper-floor mid-13th century trefoil-headed doorway has a slot for the beam securing the private door to the prior's apartments to the west. Their basement (? for storage) had a western passage. On its west wall is a small chamber with a sub-basement, beyond which a narrow channel with openings at each end served the garderobe above.

From the dormitory's south-east corner led Prior Bertram's beautiful first-floor chapel, with its interior lofty arcade of blank pointed arches divided by shafts with moulded capitals, bands, and bases.

The excavated northern buildings had been adapted later for agricultural use. Other remains, as yet unexcavated, lie to the north and east beneath farmland.

BRANCEPETH

Brancepeth lies 6 miles south-west of Durham on the A690, left and right of which lies the attractive 18th–19th-century estate village. To the left, the tree-lined street ends in park gates. Beyond them, the castle lies to the right and St Brandon's church ahead.

The Castle

Before entering, it is rewarding to walk round the outside, noting the curtain walls with sentry walks and turrets with original work on the west side.

Originally a military stronghold, it overlooks the steep ravine of Stockley Beck on the south-west and was moated on the north and east. Here, the moat later became a lake, now dry. Across the beck, the medieval bridge, rebuilt and gothicized, carried the old main road past the castle to the church and ancient village, removed when the park was created.

Brancepeth had a castle by the 12th century, when the monk Reginald wrote of a poor man released from imprisonment here by St Brandon's intervention. The Bulmers owned Brancepeth, besides the Yorkshire lands and castles of Sheriff Hutton, until Emma de Bulmer, daughter and heiress of Bertrand de Bulmer (and widow of Peter de Valoignes) married Geoffrey

Brancepeth Castle: the north front has an early 19th-century Norman style gatehouse, replacing the medieval gateway and portcullis. The chapel occupies the upper floor to the left. Groups can be taken round the castle by appointment; and tours (lasting about 50 minutes) are usually available on Monday, Tuesday, Thursday and Friday at 12 noon from the Post Office in the gatehouse. (Tel: (0191) 378 0628.) *Claughton Photography.*

Neville in 1174. The earliest surviving work is by Ralph Neville, 1st Earl of Westmorland, grandfather of Warwick the King-maker, and Marshall of England from 1399 until his death in 1425. The Nevilles owned Raby also but preferred Brancepeth.

A 16th-century description (the earliest) records two courtyards: one, largely bounded by a moat, with three lodging towers and three for ornament; the second with a pleasure garden entered by a great tower bearing a lion rampant. Ralph Neville, 4th Earl of Westmorland (1523–49), had just added new work.

The Rising of the North probably began here in 1569, and Charles, the last earl, forfeited his estates to the Crown. In 1613 James I granted Brancepeth to Robert Carr, having made him Baron Brancepeth and Earl of Somerset. Carr's steward's survey describes fine stained glass windows from Normandy with imagery and coats of arms and, in the gallery, the life of Christ.

In 1615, Carr, accused of poisoning Sir Thomas Overbury, was imprisoned and in 1629 the Brancepeth property was granted in trust for sale to certain London citizens, who conveyed it, in 1633, to Lady Middleton, Abraham Crosselis and John Jones. In 1635, the British Navy's first three-decker ship, *Sovereign of the Seas*, was built at Woolwich from 1,400 trees felled from the West Wood, across Stockley Beck, south of the castle. The estate was sold, in 1636, to Ralph Cole of Newcastle (grandson of a Gateshead blacksmith) in trust for his son, later Sir Nicholas Cole, who made it his home. His son and heir Sir Ralph, patron of the fine arts and pupil of

Van Dyck, became impoverished by keeping Italian painters at Brancepeth.

For £16,800, with a £500 annuity for himself and £200 to his wife if she survived him, he sold Brancepeth in 1701 to Sir Henry Bellasys, whose daughter in the ballad awaited 'Bobbie Shafto' of Whitworth Hall across the park. Three Bellasys generations lived here until, in 1774, Sir William's only daughter devised the castle and its estates (over 4,600 acres) to her relative, the Earl of Fauconberg. He sold them almost immediately to John Tempest of Wynyard. Sir Henry Vane-Tempest sold them in 1796 for £75,000 to William Russell, an industrialist and coal-owner who 'wrote to the end of his life like an illiterate labourer' but amassed vast wealth, bought several pocket boroughs (including Saltash and Bletchingly), managed them for the Whigs, and had political connections with Grimsby and Lincoln. His son, Major Matthew Russell (of the Militia), a huge pleasure-seeking man, immense eater and great hunter, married in 1797 Elizabeth Tennyson, aunt of the poet. Although devoted to him, she was in contrast, beautiful, charming, refined, a great reader, a writer of verse and deeply religious.

When William Russell died in June 1817, and his widow shortly after, Matthew and Elizabeth moved immediately to Brancepeth and began 'restoration' (major rebuilding) employing John Patterson, the Edinburgh architect, who favoured Norman features but had no archaeological knowledge. His huge Norman-style gatehouse with round towers replaced the medieval gateway and portcullis flanked by

Brancepeth (St Brandon): the church from the north-east; the north porch, in classical style, has doors on all four sides, and is part of John Cosin's restoration work. The interior has medieval carved canopies, recumbent effigies, magnificent 17th-century fittings, and much else of interest. It can be seen by applying to the Post Office in the Castle Gatehouse.

Claughton Photography.

square towers. He created, at the south-west corner of the courtyard, a *porte-cochère* before a great entrance hall and grand staircase leading to semi-circular galleries beneath a round sky-light, a new dining-room and service wing, the (later-named) Hamilton Tower and a state bedroom. He refitted the vaulted medieval towers: the Neville Tower (south-west) as a drawing-room, exposing a groined vault (again covered) inscribed *Mais Droyte*, and elaborately decorated in the interstices with emblems of the Order of the Garter and the Garter encircling the Neville cross; and the Bulmer Tower (really two towers) (west), with its groined vaults, as the saloon and Baron's Hall. Under each, large medieval saddle-vaulted apartments remain. In the walls are recesses of blocked windows and doorways, and under the Baron's Hall, the west end has two side rooms (one a latrine) in the wall thickness.

From the new entrance hall an armour gallery was built inside the courtyard wall, to whose exterior was added the new Russell Tower, containing a state bedroom, replacing a post-medieval building. Through the gallery, the Constable's Tower became the library, connected by a billiard room (above the old stabling) to the Westmorland Tower (east of the gate) fitted as a chapel.

These alterations cost over £120,000. Charles Tennyson (d'Eyncourt from 1835), Elizabeth's brother, acted as 'agent and arbiter', engaging a chef, butler, and 12 year old Emma Maria's governess, and helping Matthew's son William when he was in debt. In return, Matthew got Charles into Parliament. Matthew was M.P. for Durham for 15 years before he made his maiden speech, urged by Charles. However, when, in September 1819, Charles' baby son died, Matthew's letter of condolence proceeded quickly to discuss armour, historical paintings and other decorations for his 'Baronial Hall'. Stained glass windows designed by Stothard for the Neville Tower each cost £600. The finished castle was opened at Christmas 1820 with lavish festivities.

Elizabeth gave liberally to her poor Tennyson relations, and after Alfred's marriage to Emily Sellwood, on 13th June 1850, offered a honeymoon at Brancepeth. The offer was declined.

In 1828, Emma married Gustavus Frederick Hamilton, eldest son of the 6th Viscount Boyne, to whom the property passed. He was made Baron Brancepeth in 1866. Salvin (Patterson's pupil 1817–21) worked here in 1829 and again in 1864–75 when he refurbished the chapel in memory of Emma Maria, Viscountess Boyne, and was estate architect. He designed the Flagstaff Tower above the *porte-cochère* and levelled the uneven courtyard to create the present grassy slope.

When Viscount Boyne left the castle in 1922, it became the Headquarters and Museum of the Durham Light Infantry (*see also page 16*). During their occupancy, the property was sold to the Duke of Westminster; and the estate was broken up in the 1960s. Pyrex Ltd. purchased the castle, using it for research and development until Corning Glass Ltd. bought out Pyrex and sold the castle into private hands. It was purchased by Mr. and Mrs. Dobson (of Dobsons Publishers). The castle is undergoing restoration and is, at present, largely unfurnished.

St Brandon's Church

Among trees north-east of the castle stands the church. Beside its dignified gateway a stile, with steps at each side of the wall, has sides built *c.* 1665 partly of medieval grave covers, one very early. The top has a grating used to scrape muddy boots.

There was an earlier church here with a rector by 1085. It was dedicated to St Brandon or Brendon. Born in A.D. 483 in Kerry, he was one of the twelve apostles of Ireland taught by Finian the Wise at Clonard, and founded Clonfert Abbey on the Boyne. Legend says he sailed to America, and when Vikings under Eric the Red reached Florida they found Irish speaking people.

Exterior and tower

Several items of interest should be seen before entering the church: an early sundial (with missing gnomon) on the nave's south-west buttress indicates only service times; an early 13th-century sculptured stone, let into the north side of the chancel's south-east buttress, represents, in a vesica, Christ in Majesty surrounded by symbols of the evangelists (compare another in St Mary-the-Less, Durham); the medieval sanctus bell-cot on the nave's east gable; and, south of the tower, a headstone to Thomas Johnson who died in 1799, with a sculptured basket and medical instruments above an amusing four-line verse.

The unbuttressed tower of three stages was begun *c.* 1250. The first floor has small round-headed windows to north and west. With the tower arch and two western bays of the nave arcades, this is the earliest part of the present building. The two storeys above have pairs of Early English lancets on each side. The belfry has a two-light window and contains eight bells given by the 8th Viscount Boyne. They replace an older peal of six, three of which were inscribed and presented in 1632 by John Cosin, bishop of Durham 1660–72, and an active rector here 1626–40 until he was exiled during the Commonwealth. Access to the belfry is by an old 'cat-ladder' made from squared timbers sawn diagonally and nailed across an oak beam. Below the parapet several corbels are carved with heads and on one is a shield charged with the Neville saltire. The ground floor west window is 19th-century.

The classical-style north entrance porch, added by John Cosin, bears the fret from his coat of arms and cherubs' heads. It has three doorways with pilasters and Ionic capitals and a curious parapet. The west doorway is now blocked. The south porch, rarely used, was built in 1892 to commemorate the Reverend R. D. Shafto's forty years as rector.

The Interior

The furnishings, mostly by Cosin, are a surprise. Their unforgettable impact distracts from the earlier architecture.

The nave's two western bays (*c.* 1250) have pointed arches on octagonal piers, bases and capitals. The north central capital has large dog-tooth mouldings and the south a smaller version. The circular font on its Frosterley marble pillar is also of this period. The contemporary chancel arch and south door are not in their original positions.

Early 14th century

Ralph, Lord Neville enlarged the church, probably in memory of his son Robert (called the 'Peacock of the North'), who slew Richard Fitz Marmaduke, Lord of Horden on Framwellgate Bridge, and was himself killed at Berwick in 1319. He widened the aisles, carried them west to engage the tower, and reset their west windows. He moved the chancel arch eastward to allow for north and south transepts. The responds made to receive their entrance arches, not built, still remain. The north transept held a cross-legged effigy 7 ft 9 in. long and 2 ft across the shoulders, representing Robert Neville. During 19th-century 'restoration' it was moved to the chancel (north side). He wears chain mail with knee-length surcoat. His heater-shaped shield bears the Neville saltire with a label of cadency. Two small figures read from books beside two head-cushions supported by six lions, and a great lion with an oak branch under its side supports the feet. By one leg lies a muzzled small dog, and under the other a dragon bites his sword point. The remaining space is filled with bold conventional flowers.

The north aisle windows are copies of the originals, while those of the south aisle are 19th-century replacements. In the north transept the east window copies the original, but the north window is 19th-century work. Both south transept windows have three lights and are of good Decorated style. The east one looks into a later Neville chapel.

About 1375, the present chancel and north and south chapels were built. All their windows and tracery have been restored in their original style. The five-light east window style is transitional between Decorated and Perpendicular, and the three-light north and south windows, three on each side, are of the same style.

The north chapel (later a vestry), entered through a pointed arch and original door, has an east two-light square-headed window (above an early exterior string-course terminating in leaf ornament), and a north three-light window under a segmented arch, both earlier than the vestry and reset from elsewhere. From the south wall a hagioscope commands the altar and a stone basin in the west wall drains into the churchyard.

The nave roof was heightened and the clerestory built. The Neville chapel or Lady's Porch lies through a wide arch in the chancel's south wall. It contained formerly two altar tombs. One, of Matilda Countess of Westmorland, with quatre-foil side panels, with shields formerly painted and the Neville saltire, was removed in 1876 to the tower base; another, in the centre, but uninscribed, was destroyed. The wood funeral helmet, once carried on coffins and now near the north door, formerly hung here. The chapel, cleared except for a tomb slab left in the floor, became the organ chamber until the organ was moved recently to the south aisle's west end. The Neville chapel has been refurbished with a glazed screen towards the chancel, backing an altar table made by Robert Thompson of Kilburn from a fine 14th-century Flemish chest, carved with foliage, tracery and grotesque figures, formerly kept in this chapel.

Brancepeth Church: view from South Aisle.

Martin Roberts.

The once 'high tomb' in the chancel has lost its sides, leaving only the plinth and the niches above it. The effigies, each cut from a single piece of oak and originally painted and gilded, are those of Ralph Neville, 2nd Earl of Westmorland and his second wife Margaret, daughter of Reginald, Lord Cobham. The knight wears armour 100 years out of date, and presenting technical problems, but his visor is up, showing his face. Lady Margaret wears a high head-dress, a very low-necked kirtle with tight mitten sleeves and a side-less surcoat deeply faced (with fur?). Both figures wear decorated collars, his with the white rose of York from which hangs the white boar, Richard III's device, and hers made of suns and roses, with a lozenge-shaped pendant jewel set in gold. From her loose girdle an aulmonière hangs on a chain.

The 15th-century nave roof has principals cusped into a trefoil arch and resting on corbels. Above them are carved figures: a bull on the north and an angel on the south each bear a shield with the Neville arms; three angels hold musical instruments; five hold shields, now plain; four are grotesque carvings or simple bosses; carved at the apex of the arches of the trusses are, west to east: 1 and 2, bosses of foliage; 3, a grotesque head; 4, a boss; 5, a head of Christ with a nimbus; 6, an angel with shield; 7, Christ seated with both hands raised.

Above the chancel arch hang two large panelled canopies. The upper set was the medieval rood screen canopy here before Cosin introduced the present screen. Twelve panels in two rows the exact width of the nave are surmounted by the Royal Arms flanked by the Yorkist white rose and the Scottish thistle. Above the top panels are (north to south): 1, a shield, argent, bearing St George's Cross, gules; 2 and 3, bosses; 4, a shield with the sacred heart, hands and feet, gules; 5 and 6, bosses; 7, gules a cross patonce argent. On square bosses in the centre row are emblems of the crucifixion: the seamless coat, nails, crown of thorns, hammer and pincers, ladder, etc. (one is lacking, and another indecipherable). The lower row has three more shields: 1, the Neville saltire; 2, party per pale gules and sable a Stafford knot argent; and 3, the bull's head crest of the Nevilles. The Stafford knot dates the panels before 1400. Margaret, first wife of the 1st Earl of Westmorland was daughter of Hugh, Earl of Stafford. She died in 1370. (Signs of the rood loft stair remain north of the chancel arch.)

The lower one, now painted white, comprises twenty-seven almost square oak panels of very intricate geometrical tracery, no two alike. Small ribs divide the designs, sunk only one quarter of an inch deep, in each panel. Moulded ribs, formerly pale blue, divide the panels from each other. At the intersections are small bosses: on one a Gothic M and on another XPC (for the Greek *Christos*). The bosses and beautiful cresting above were once gilded. The canopy came probably from the Jesus (nave) altar in Durham Cathedral, rescued by George Cliffe, one of the last monks, who became a prebendary and was rector of Brancepeth 1571–84.

He may have brought also four 15th-century panels from another screen which now forms the reredos and flank the altar. The upper parts have beautiful tracery; one panel has a shield charged with Prior Castell's badge (a winged and pierced heart); and in another is tracery formed of thistle flowers and leaves. The panels formed a dado on the south side of the Neville chapel until it was cleared in 1876.

The 17th century

John Cosin became rector in 1626 and had installed magnificent woodwork before 1633, when Newcastle churchwardens with five carpenters visited here. His distinctive styles, better known in Durham Cathedral and Castle, and in Auckland Castle chapel, are concentrated here in an almost completely surviving interior deserving detailed attention. His coat of arms, a gold fret on a blue ground, appears frequently to mark his work.

The chancel, inspired by medieval originals, has some similarities to Sedgefield. The flat ceiling is decorated as a tester or canopy and panelled in squares arranged diagonally with bosses or angels at the junctions. Over the sanctuary, with its massive six-legged Communion Table given by Cosin in 1628, angels bear shields with inscriptions praising God. Those in black letter read: S'ctus, Sanctus, S'ctus (Holy, Holy, Holy); and D'nus Deus O'ip't'ns (Lord God Omnipotent); and in roman letters: GLORIA DEO IN EXCELSIS (Glory to God in the highest); NON NOBIS D'NE (Not unto us O Lord); SED NOM'I TUO (but to thy Name). Other shields bear crosses of St George and St Edward. The Communion rail is like that at Haughton-le-Skerne. The then familiar concept of a monarch holding court beneath a canopy or tester and separated from others by a rail is

St Brandon's Church: Neville recumbent effigies in north transept.   *Claughton Photography.*

carried here into the idea of God's majesty, with his throne represented by the altar table.

The magnificently carved oak chancel screen, in five divisions and with soaring pinnacles, is an excellent copy of Perpendicular work in a style reminiscent of the Caen stone Neville screen behind the high altar of Durham Cathedral. The upper parts of the screen gates are filled with tracery. Five chancel stalls on each side stand beneath continuous canopies against high panelling, while of three more, on either side returned against the screen, the two nearest the gates have separate canopies. All the seats have misereres carved with foliage. The chancel stalls were intended for communicants who moved here at the words of invitation during the service. (Robed choirs were introduced into parish churches in the 19th century, imitating cathedrals, the earliest probably being that at Leeds in 1843.)

On the north wall a large blank tablet with classic pilasters and with fruit swags was intended as Cosin's memorial but never completed. As Bishop of Durham from 1660 he was buried in Auckland Castle chapel.

The hagioscopes in either side of the chancel arch were inserted so that worshippers in the aisles could see the altar.

Just as at this period the chancel seating was reserved for communicants, so parts of the nave were especially allocated. A pew plan of 1639 shows the Brancepeth arrangements. Males sat in the centre and their female relatives in the aisles. At the west end, seats near the font were reserved for baptisms.

On each side of the chancel arch against the easternmost pillars of the nave stood twin pulpits of equal height, the prayer and reading 'pew' on the south and the pulpit on the north, each with its clerk's desk in front. George Herbert installed similar twin pulpits at Leighton Bromswold (Huntingdonshire) in 1627, making the famous remark that 'they should neither have a precedence or priority of the other, but that prayer and preaching, being equally useful, might agree like brethren, and have an equal honour and estimation'.

The reading 'pew' with its square sounding board and elaborate canopy, was moved to the north side of the chancel arch in the 19th-century 'restoration' to serve as a pulpit for preaching, but its twin perished, to be replaced by an eagle lectern. The pulpit's richly carved acanthus frieze, cherubs' heads and feminine motifs are characteristic of Cosin's later work elsewhere.

On the south side of the crossing, facing the centre aisle, stands the large castle pew, with an oak framework to carry curtains against draughts and servant seats behind. The Rectory family occupied similar seats opposite.

In the nave, the pew ends terminate in carved 'poppy heads' above rusticated bases and strapwork exactly like that at Haughton-le-Skerne. The pew floors, raised a step above the flagged floor, were eighteen inches high from the aisle until lowered in the 'restorations'.

Parish records give the date 1638 when the timber was sawn for the middle alley, and the craftsman's name: Robert Barker.

The font canopy, now carried on four wrought iron posts designed in 1972 by George Pace, is poorly carved in comparison with Cosin's other work. It has a tall crocketed spire on Corinthian columns with flat tracery between, decorated with crowns and cherubs' heads, and with a dove, symbol of the Holy Ghost, in the finial. The text round the hexagonal base is: 'Be baptised – and you shall – receive the – gift of the – Holy Ghost. – Acts 2v. 38th.' [i.e. Acts 2: 38.]

The clock face above the tower arch was left there when its works inside the tower ceased to function. Originally it bore the arms of both Calverley and Jennings, Cosin's parishioners. There is a Calverley vault in the chancel.

Cosin embellished his buildings with stained glass; but all that remains here is a roundel of Flemish glass in the north aisle.

Most of the alterations and 'restoration' were carried out in 1864 at the expense of the 7th Viscount Boyne and his wife Emma Maria, grand-daughter of William Russell.

BURN HALL

Burn Hall lies 2–3 miles due south of Durham and west of A167.

The manor of Burn Hall or Burnehall (perhaps so called from its proximity to the River Browney) was part of the estate of the Nevilles of Brancepeth Castle until the end of the 13th century, when

Burn Hall: built in 1821 to the design of Ignatius Bonomi, it stands on high ground commanding lawns, woods and water. It was bought in 1926 by the Mill Hill Missionaries. In late 1995 it was bought by a housing trust for conversion into private residences. *Durham County Council.*

Robert de Neville released suit of court at Brancepeth to Isabella de Brackenbury, who married Peter de Neville.

Through marriage between Maud (born c. 1355) and Sir John Claxton, the estate passed to the Claxtons whose manor house stood on high ground above the Browney bridge, a site overlooking the present hall. Robert Claxton, the last of this family to hold Burnehall, supported the rebellion of the Northern Earls, but saved both life and property through his wife's sister's intervention. Afterwards, owing to great financial difficulties, he sold the manor to George Lawson of Little Usworth, who provided in his will for Robert to recover it within a year after his death (in 1587), on payment of £2,000. Robert was unable to fulfil the condition and through Thomas Lawson, George's son and heir, a number of non-resident proprietors acquired interests in the estate. Among them was Dorothy, daughter of Sir Henry Constable, of Burton Constable, in Holderness, who married his relative Roger Lawson of Heaton and of the Inner Temple, son of Sir Ralph Lawson of Brough Hall, Yorkshire. Burn Hall occurs in her marriage settlement of 10th March 1598. Meantime the old Claxton house seems to have become ruinous. The property was conveyed in 1621 to Christopher Peacock of Richmond. Simon Peacock IV, living at Burn Hall in 1689, died in January 1708, and his son sold Old Burnhall (the estate east of the road) in 1715 to Posthumous Smith, LL.D. (d. 1725), Commissary General and Official to the Archdeacon of Durham, and his son-in-law Sir George Wheler, the traveller and scholar.

In 1717, New Burnhall was bought by his nephew George Smith, son of the Reverend Dr John Smith (canon of Durham, and scholar, noted especially for his fine edition of *Bede's Historic Works*, which long remained unsurpassed). George Smith refused to take the Oath of Allegiance to William and Mary, took Orders in the Non-Juring Church and became titular Bishop of Durham. The memorial to George Smith, who died in 1756, is at the east end of the south aisle of St Oswald's, Durham. The residence of the Smiths, to quote a contemporary description, stood 'low and sequestered, close on the water of Browney, which forms a long silvery canal, beautifully fringed with oak and alder'. His son predeceased him in 1752, aged 29, leaving a son, George, who was living at Burn Hall in 1789.

Sir John Soane prepared designs for George Smith in 1784, but only the Home Farm was erected in 1786. The splendid cow-house, recently restored for residential use, has a central pavilion with high arched entrance and pediments, flanked by diagonally placed wings, each with three arches, and terminating in small pavilions with pyramid roofs. Behind is a round bull house.

Before 1813, George Smith sold the property to Bryan John Salvin, younger son of William Salvin of Croxdale Hall. He commissioned the present mansion and died in 1842. It was built in 1821 by Moody, the builder of Ushaw College, and completed in 1834 for £30,000 to the design of Ignatius Bonomi. The imposing front has a huge central Ionic portico of four columns, with an inner projecting porch, and four bays on each side. The façade is rusticated, with strong bands, surmounted by a parapet and balustrade in panels, while the roof is of French mansard type. In the large entrance hall, the elegant staircase rises in a single flight in a rear semi-circular projection, before dividing into two.

A conservatory, costing a further £2,000, stands on the Browney on low ground near the site of the earlier house whose stones adorn a rockery.

When Marmaduke Henry Salvin died in 1924, Burn Hall was offered for sale by his trustee, Major Salvin of Croxdale. A Roman Catholic, he sold the mansion for £5,000, with 60 acres of surrounding land with the Home Farm for a further £3,000, to the Mill Hill Fathers (St Joseph's Society for Foreign Missions) to found a junior seminary where boys would be encouraged to become missionary priests. As the hall is built on a pillar of coal, mineral rights were included in the sale to prevent mining subsidence; and 10 acres were added on the opposite bank of the Browney to ensure privacy.

St Joseph's College opened in 1926, with nuns of the Franciscan Missionaries of St Joseph to look after the boys. In 1954, a small wing was added at the back, as a Convent to which the sisters moved from hitherto cramped quarters.

Burn Hall Home Farm: the late eighteenth-century Byre and Long Barn designed by Sir John Soane. *Claughton Photography.*

Junior seminaries fell from favour and St Joseph's College closed in 1972. Its accommodation became available for retreats, quiet days, seminars, and other activities. The Convent closed in 1976, owing to falling numbers, and after standing empty for four years, was refurbished and opened in 1982 as St Joseph's House of Prayer, offering also the *Poustinia* (Russian for 'desert'), a room for a solitary retreat.

More recently, the Minsteracres Monastery Trust developed projects here for handicapped trainees.

In an increasingly ecumenical climate, Burn Hall offered facilities to non-Roman Catholics. Anglican, Baptist, Quaker and United Reformed groups, besides the Samaritans and secular organisations used it.

Provided permission was obtained from the Rector, visitors were welcome to the grounds, especially attractive in spring, with their gardens, woodland walks and cemetery by the Browney.

The Mill Hill Missionaries left Burn Hall on 29th August 1995. The Hall and surrounding grounds were sold to Troveworth Residential Ltd., Durham City, for conversion into ten private residences. All facilities for retreats, House of Prayer, and other activities are no longer on offer. The missionaries, a community of four, now occupy and own the byre and long barn designed by Sir John Soane as part of the Home Farm buildings. These, with the surrounding fields and woodland behind the houses, as well as the buildings on the left of the Soane Byre, all belong to the missionaries and are no longer part of the Burn Hall Estate.

BISHOP AUCKLAND

Auckland Castle and the Bishops' Park

Auckland Castle lies at the east end of the Market Place. It became the only residence of the bishops of Durham when Bishop Van Mildert, last of the Prince-Bishops, gave up Durham Castle in 1832 to found Durham University. Its massive gateway, crowned by a pinnacled clock turret, was designed *c.* 1760 by Sir Thomas Robinson for Bishop Richard Trevor. The Elizabethan-style lodge within is a century later.

Durham bishops probably had a residence at Auckland before the Norman Conquest. A 10th-century grant of 'two Aclits' to the church of Durham refers to West Auckland and St Andrew Auckland (South Church), which had a pre-Conquest church. Bishop Auckland grew up later beside the episcopal manor house, where Bishop Hugh of Le Puiset built a hall about 1183. It was never fortified; but Bishop Hatfield called it a *castrum* (fortified building) in 1346, when the English army camped in the park on the night before the Battle of Neville's Cross.

A north gatehouse, built by Bishop Skirlaw (1388–1406), was convenient for access from St Andrew Auckland, a mile to the north-west; it may have led into a courtyard behind the gallery wing called Scotland (left of the present entrance), erected to lodge Scottish hostages sent occasionally by the king into the bishops' custody. (Skirlaw also built Auckland Bridge, on the Wolsingham road.)

The long straight drive, beside a low arcaded wall, passes the south end of the north–south wing to the

Auckland Castle: tripartite entrance screen. The Chapel, State Rooms (including the Throne Room), medieval kitchens with an exhibition on the life of St Cuthbert and the history of Durham Diocese, are open May to September on Sundays, Tuesdays, Wednesdays, and Thursdays 2 p.m.–5 p.m.; Bank Holiday Mondays and Saturdays 2 p.m.–5 p.m. in August. Last admissions 30 minutes before closing time. Groups and school visits by arrangement throughout the year. (Tel: (01388) 601627.)

Claughton Photography.

recessed three-arched crenellated gateway to the Castle itself. It was designed by James Wyatt for Bishop Barrington whose coat of arms, with those of the diocese, decorate the centre arch. The drive terminates in the beautiful Bishops' Park.

The medieval Castle has been extended and adapted. After the Civil War, Parliament confiscated and sold it as church property c. 1650 to Sir Arthur Haslerigg for £6102 8s. 11½d. An inventory made for him lists courts, yards and gardens totalling 6 acres within an encircling wall still partly embattled. He demolished the chapel to re-use the materials for a new mansion in the grounds, probably never finished. Other buildings fell into decay. At the restoration of the monarchy, church property was returned to its owners and Haslerigg was sent to the Tower.

Bishop John Cosin (1660–72) restored the Castle; but Bishop Barrington (1791–1826) with his architect James Wyatt made subsequent alterations.

The entrance

Bishop Barrington's ornate entrance porch of 1794 leads into a vestibule created by Bishop Cosin to link the chapel with the domestic buildings.

The State and Domestic apartments

The Entrance or Gentlemen's Hall

The oldest surviving part of the north–south two-storey wing built by Bishop Antony Bek (1283–1312) (whose short sword is still at the Castle), is the entrance hall left of the vestibule. It was restored by Bishop Cosin, whose coat of arms appears in the window glass; but the architect James Wyatt transformed it for Bishop Barrington (1791–1826), by removing the west wall to insert his elegant staircase, and covering the early massive oak beams with an ornate false Gothic ceiling. Shields bearing the coats of arms of other English dioceses hang high on the walls. Former bishops left items here, including the stuffed snowy-owl which failed to discourage the many bats in the chapel.

To the left, in the great kitchen, where massive pillars support the great chamber above, a colourful exhibition tells the story of St Cuthbert and the history of Durham Diocese.

The staircase divides after the first flight, the right branch mounting to a window overlooking the Wear valley and the route of the original entrance road. The landing leads past a large tapestry, and the head of the left stair, to the ante-chamber and Throne Room, created from the seventy-six feet long medieval great common room.

The ante-chamber

In this elegant octagonal room, visitors once awaited an audience with the bishop. Over a doorway on the left, leading to the Victoria wing (occupied by Queen Victoria when travelling north) hangs a portrait of Bishop Thomas Wolsey (1523–80), who never visited his diocese. George Richmond's two pastel-chalk drawings of Montague Villiers and his wife hang in this room: he was bishop only for the year 1860. On the right, the large window overlooks Scotland and the kitchen garden, where the right-hand south-facing wall once carried heating pipes to ripen peaches. Slender double doors with fine brass work lead into the Throne Room.

The Throne Room

At the south end, the central arch of an elaborate plaster screen frames the bishop's throne. Above are the arms of the diocese impaled with those of Bishop Barrington, surmounted by a ducal coronet and mitre with a crook and sword, signifying the temporal, spiritual and pastoral office of the Prince-Bishops.

Here, as the monarch's representative, bishops received the sons and daughters of northern nobility, to save the long and hazardous journey to London to be presented at court. James Wyatt tinted the south-facing Gothic windows pink and green 'to make the ladies appear less pale in the bright sunlight'.

Former bishops' portraits look down from the walls. Bishop John Cosin, restorer of Auckland Castle, hangs to the right of the fireplace, while on the left is Bishop Van Mildert (who died in 1836), last of the Prince-Bishops. A former bishop brought from Thomas Becket's shrine at Canterbury the marble tops of the two gilt tables flanking the fireplace. A carved door to the right of the throne leads to another state room.

The 16th-century addition

Bishop Thomas Ruthall (1509–22) began to extend Bek's buildings southwards, with an oriel of two storeys next to his great chamber. It contains the long dining-room above the former servants' hall, made into the library in the early 20th century. Bishop Tunstall's device of a curry comb with bird supporters decorates the ceiling of the raised window bay, and Bishop Ruthall's coat of arms appears over the lower oriel. Next, over the stone entrance hall, is the chamber later known as the King Charles Room. Bishop Tunstal (1529–59) completed the work by 1530.

The dining-room

This apartment is almost the same size as the Throne Room. Bishop Trevor's coloured coat of arms is in the centre of the moulded ceiling of 1760. The inlaid African ebony table extends to four times its present size; and Bishop Barrington's coat of arms decorates the scrolled tops of the rosewood chairs. Wyatt designed the three side-tables. Thirteen priceless paintings of 1640, each 8 feet tall, and by the Spaniard Francesco Zurburán, represent Jacob and his twelve sons. Bishop Trevor bought them for £124 after pirates captured them on their way to South America.

The King Charles Room

Charles I slept here when travelling to and from Scotland, the last time as a prisoner being taken to London for trial and execution.

This is the family dining-room on special occasions, and is not usually shown to visitors. The fireplace, in the Grinling Gibbons style, has a charming central sculpture of two children and a bird's nest. The rococo ceiling carries Bishop Trevor's badge: a dragon sitting on a bishop's hat. He bought Vecchio's *Judgement of Solomon*, the copy of Paolo Veronese's *Wedding Feast at Cana in Galilee*, and the four evangelists, painted on wood by G. Lanfranco, in the corners.

The Chapel

A chapel existed by 1271, but Bishop Antony Bek (1283–1312), is said to have built a new one of two storeys. Probably he added to the existing chapel the upper storey known as the high chapel. It stood parallel to the south side of the great hall until c. 1650, when Haslerigg, the Commonwealth lay owner, demolished it, intending to use its materials to build a new house, possibly never finished. The original chapel outline is visible in the grass in dry summers.

Bishop Hugh of Le Puiset built the great aisled hall (now the chapel). Four-shafted columns, two of sandstone and two of Frosterley marble, carry the arcades. The east wall had three doorways (now blocked) leading down steps to kitchen, buttery, pantry, and other domestic offices. Two blocked doorways in the north wall's eastern bay are visible externally. The lower one was the north entrance to the screens passage, while the higher one led to the musicians' gallery above. The dais and high table occupied the hall's west end adjacent to the bishop's private apartments. A central open hearth, with its smoke louvre above, provided heating. The windows of the north and south aisles, the east ends of the aisles, and the west end of the nave, are ascribed to Bishop Hatfield (1345–81).

When Bishop John Cosin (1660–71) destroyed Haslerigg's work and restored the property, he spent large sums, especially in converting the great hall into St Peter's chapel, and connecting it to the main house on the west by a short wing. The outer doors, the ante-chapel door, and the chapel's western screens all display Cosin's distinctive style of woodwork.

Above the north and south arcades he built a high clerestory to give lightness and loftiness, heightening the roof to 64 feet, and raising the floor in black and white marble; and his are the white marble sanctuary steps. Above the Holy Table hung a tapestry (since removed) representing Solomon's meeting with the Queen of Sheba. Cosin's ceiling displays his coat of arms (a gold fret on blue) and the arms of the diocese in gold, blue and silver, in alternate squares, painted by Van Eersell who worked also in Durham Castle and Bishop Cosin's Library. The central panel is flanked by cherubs, mitres and eagles. Cosin's coat of arms once also decorated the window glass. He was buried in the central aisle beneath the epitaph he composed.

His successor, Bishop Nathaniel Crewe, gave the Father Schmidt organ (with black and white keys reversed) for the west gallery in 1688. Bishop Van Mildert (1826–36) carried out extensive repairs, marked by his own arms cut occasionally into Cosin's woodwork.

Bishop Joseph Barber Lightfoot (1879–89) restored the chapel, adding a new oak Holy Table with cedar panels; a carved dark Frosterley marble reredos with oak above; the credence table (part of an ancient altar slab found in the house); the six angels standing on the corbels which supported the roof of the original hall; and the heraldic shields round the walls. Both at the east end, and from six windows east of the screen, he removed the inferior glass which had gradually replaced that of Cosin. He planned the present windows to describe the spread of the Christian faith from New Testament times, continuing through the Northumbrian saints, and descending to the See of Durham, naming later bishops.

To the chapel re-dedication he invited fifty-seven Bishops, recording their names on brass plates flanking the doorway beneath the organ gallery. He died the next year and is buried in front of the sanctuary.

Joseph Nollekens' monument to Bishop Richard Trevor (d. 1771) is in the south-west corner of the ante-chapel.

The Bishop's Park

From the three-fold Castle entrance, the long arcaded wall beside the drive continues to the beautifully wooded and undulating Bishops' Park of

The Bishop's Park: eighteenth-century deer cote. The park is open daily from 7 a.m. to sunset. *Claughton Photography.*

Auckland Castle: the chapel ceiling. Alternate squares display Cosin's coat of arms (a gold fret on blue) and the arms of the diocese. The central panel is flanked by eagles. *Claughton Photography.*

800 acres with its excellent picnic areas. The River Gaunless (the 'loiterer') winds across its south side to meet the River Wear just beyond the Castle's outer wall near the Binchester road.

Like the Castle, the park is owned by the Church Commissioners; it is open to the public except for parts leased to local farmers and to Bishop Auckland Golf Club.

Boldon Book (1183) recorded the park, where, as in other medieval parks, wild animals were driven within its ditch and paling to be hunted for food when needed. Bishop Philip of Poitou enlarged it by 1200. After the English army camped here on the night before the Battle of Neville's Cross in 1346, and perhaps to repair the depredations of the troops, Bishop Hatfield newly walled it in stone for £40 in 1349. Deer are mentioned in 1394, and Leland wrote of 'fallow dere and wild beasts' in 1587. A 1627 Survey records 'wilde kyne with calves and bulls, etc., of all sortes'; and in 1634 they were said to be 'white' and could be 'violent and furious'. All had been exterminated before the Parliamentary Survey of 1647.

At the Restoration, Bishop Cosin re-stocked the park and had Park Keepers; and Bishop Joseph Butler (1750–2) seems to have extended it and rebuilt its ruinous walls.

In 1760 Bishop Richard Trevor built a large deer cote (now in the care of English Heritage) with a grassed quadrangle within arcades to shelter fallow deer. The tower on its east side once had an upper room where the Bishop and his guests could rest during hunting expeditions. In 1852 there were about 300 deer; and deer roamed the park more recently. Sadly, there are none today.

CHESTER-LE-STREET

St Mary and St Cuthbert's Church

The church was built on the site of a Roman fort (*Concangium*) and began as the seat of the Bishop of Lindisfarne from 882. Here, the Congregation of St Cuthbert settled after the Viking raids on the north-east coast, before finally moving to Durham in 995. The present church, mostly of the 13th-century, contains a remarkable series of fourteen monumental effigies, mostly placed here in the late 16th century by John, Lord Lumley, to commemorate his ancestors.

The Anker's House

The western bay of the north aisle has been walled off to form the two rooms of the Anchorage, or Anker House, one above the other; and two similar rooms, connecting with them, were built outside the aisle. A recluse or anchorite lived here from the 1380s, spending his time in prayer and meditation, the earliest known being John Wessyngton. After the Reformation it became a small almshouse. In 1986, the Anker's House became an attractive museum of the town's history and church treasures from Roman times onwards, receiving honourable mention in the Museum of the Year Awards.

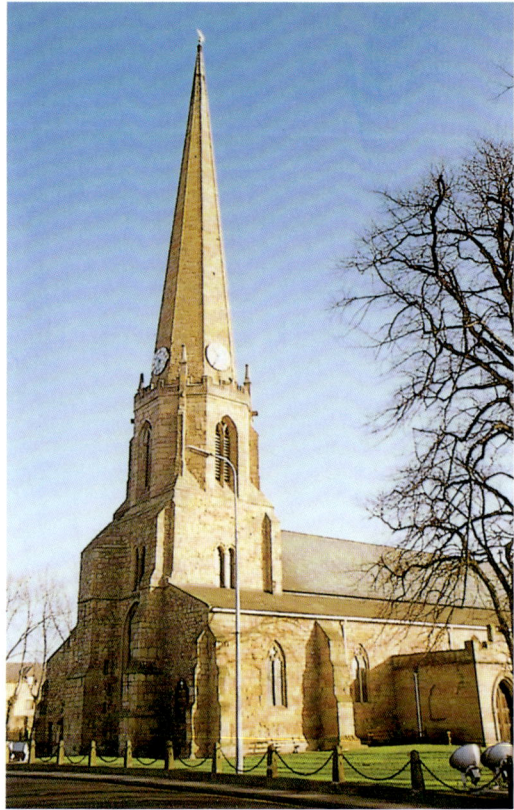

Chester-le-Street, St Mary and St Cuthbert: the west end with the Anker's House, right. Open: April to October, Mondays to Saturdays and Bank Holidays 10 a.m.–3.30 p.m. Closed Sundays, but church open for services. (Tel: (0191) 388 3295.)   *H. MacBride.*

MONKWEARMOUTH
St Peter's Church

Monkwearmouth is now part of Sunderland. Here, on the north bank of the Wear, Benedict Biscop founded a monastery on land granted by Ecgfrith, King of Northumbria, in 675. This was followed by its 'twin' at Jarrow in 684. St Peter's west wall originally had a doorway at its south end (perhaps beside a west altar), blocked when a little later a central door and porch were added, the latter the burial place of Eosterwine (*d.* 685), the first abbot appointed by Biscop. The porch has arched openings with baluster shafts decorated with intertwined creatures; above are faint traces of a large figure sculptured in relief. The fourth stage and belfry of the tower are late pre-Conquest.

The church had an eastern apse and north and south porticus (side-chambers of Anglo-Saxon type), but was rebuilt in the 14th century. The north aisle was added in 1874 to meet the needs of a rising population. The Anglo-Saxon monastic site south of the church has been extensively excavated. The Venerable Bede began here his monastic life and the famous *Codex Amiatinus* and other manuscripts were written here. St Peter's became a cell of Durham Priory after the Norman conquest. St. Peter's has a visitor centre displaying excavation finds and a descriptive video.

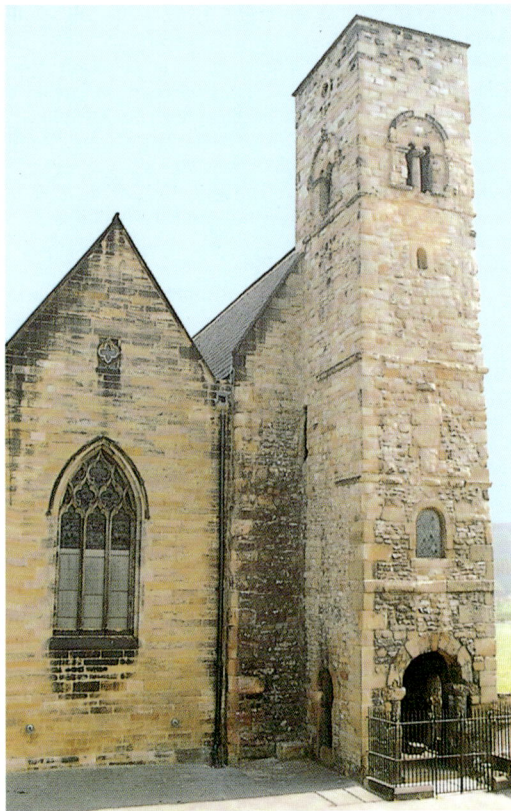

Monkwearmouth, St Peter: right, the 7th-century low tower and porch and above, two late pre-Conquest upper storeys. Open: Weekdays 2 to 4.30 p.m., Easter to 31 October. Conducted tours; large parties should book in advance. (Tel: (0191) 567 3726 or (0191) 564 0431 during opening hours.)
G. Dresser.

JARROW:
ST PAUL'S AND BEDE'S WORLD

The church, the monastic site, and Bede's World lie together 10 miles from Newcastle off the A19 (exit at the south end of the Tyne Tunnel).

St Paul's parish church has been used for worship for thirteen centuries. Its chancel was the smaller of two Anglo-Saxon monastic churches on the same east-west axis; and its present nave and north aisle (1866) stand on the site of a larger church, which was decorated richly with early sculpture now on display. The foundation stone is set into the chancel arch facing the present nave. Each May, the church holds an annual lecture on Bede and his times by a distinguished scholar.

The adjacent Anglo-Saxon monastic site on the banks of the River Don has been excavated, its plan laid out, and the later Norman monastic ruins conserved. An excellent model of the Anglo-Saxon monastery may be seen in Jarrow Hall.

Bede's World is a striking new museum designed by award-winning architects. This, and the **Georgian Jarrow Hall**, display Northumbria's early history and explore the remarkable achievements of the life and times of the Venerable Bede (673–735), the renowned monk, scholar, prolific writer and teacher.

He was called the 'father of English historians' from his fame as author of *The History of the English Church and People*. Jarrow, the twin monastery of St Peter's Monkwearmouth, was internationally famous in Bede's day as a centre of Christian learning. Bede's remains lie in Durham Cathedral.

After the Norman conquest, Jarrow became a cell of Durham Priory.

Jarrow, St Paul: the eastern of the two Anglo-Saxon monastic churches where Bede worshipped, and now the chancel of the later church. *Bede's World.*

Gyrwe, Jarrow's name in Bede's day, brings to life the world he knew, with its timber buildings under construction, its farming methods, crops and animals. The River Don, once a natural harbour, is landscaped to restore inter-tidal mud-flats as a habitat for wading birds.

St Paul's, with its associated sites, is being revived today as a centre of historical, religious and cultural importance.

Amenities include a gift shop; a restaurant serving home-made fare; temporary exhibitions and events; small conference or meeting facilities; ample free parking.

Open: April to October: Tuesday to Saturday 10 a.m. to 5.30 p.m., Sundays and Bank Holidays, 12 noon to 5.30 p.m.; November to March: Tuesday to Saturday 11 a.m. to 4.30 p.m., Sundays 12 noon to 5.30 p.m. Usually closed Christmas to New Year. (Tel: (0191) 489 2106. Fax: (0191) 428 2361.)

RABY CASTLE

Raby, one of the most magnificent medieval castles in the country, is said to be on the site of the Staindrop mansion of King Cnut (995–1036). Bertram de Bulmer (of Brancepeth and Sheriff Hutton) was grandfather of the Norman heiress, Isabel Neville, who married the Lord of Raby and gave the name Neville to their descendants. Raby has a distinguished history. Joan Beaumont, John of Gaunt's daughter and the king's sister, was the second wife of Ralph Neville, 1st Earl of Westmorland, the mother of Cicely Neville, the 'Rose of Raby'. Cicely married Richard Plantaganet, Duke of York, and was the mother of Edward IV and Richard III. On 13th November 1569 in the Barons'

Raby Castle: the south front reflected in the lake within the deer park. Open: Easter Saturday–Wednesday; closed rest of April; May and June, Wednesdays and Sundays only; July, August and September, daily except Saturdays; also Bank Holiday weekends Saturdays–Wednesdays. Castle: 1–5 p.m.; park and gardens 11 a.m.–5.30 p.m. Charges: Castle, gardens and coach houses: adults £4, children £1·50, over 60s £3, family ticket (2 adults and up to 3 children) £10; Gardens and coach houses only: adults £1·50, children and over 60s £1. No photography or video-filming inside castle; no dogs except on leads in Park. Carriage and fire engine collection; tea rooms; car park. Enquiries: (Tel: (01833) 660202.)

Claughton Photography.

Hall, the northern nobles and gentry plotted the fatal Rising of the North, when the Crown confiscated the castle and Raby estates. After 43 years under the charge of a Keeper, Sir Henry Vane bought Raby and Barnard, and twice received Charles I at Raby.

The castle has magnificent apartments with fine paintings, furniture and porcelain, and a 14th-century kitchen. There are 10 acres of gardens; and the park of 270 acres (exclusive of enclosed woodlands) contains two herds of deer, one of red deer and the other of fallow. Raby is the seat of Harry John Neville, 11th Lord Barnard, who was appointed Lord Lieutenant of County Durham in 1970. He is descended from both the Vanes and the Nevilles.

ESCOMB CHURCH

One and a half miles west of Bishop Auckland, and built probably between 670 and 690 from Roman stones, the church stands in a roughly circular churchyard suggesting possibly a Celtic religious site, now hallowed by thirteen centuries of Christian worship. Do not fail to walk round the outside first. The church exterior, thirty-six feet high, and narrower at the top, was originally plastered. There was once a western annexe, matching the chancel in size. The austere north side is unaltered Saxon work and contains a rosette from a Roman altar. The blocked north doorway has a single stone lintel and massive 'long and short' stone jambs leaning towards each other. A similar blocked doorway led from the chancel into a former Saxon *porticus* or side-chamber. Beside it, a reversed Roman stone is inscribed LEG VI (the sixth legion). The western annexe and *porticus* were excavated in 1968. Under the former

Escomb Church: this 7th-century Saxon church is one of the finest examples of early Christian architecture in northern Europe. Open: summer 9 a.m.–8 p.m.; winter 9 a.m.–4 p.m. Admission free. Guided tours and special services available by arrangement with the vicar. (Tel: (01388) 602861); other enquiries to Tourist Secretary: (01388) 662265.) *Margot Johnson.*

were burials pre-dating the annexe; and Saxon window glass like that at Jarrow was found on the *porticus* site. High on the south wall is a Saxon sundial whose three lines mark the hours of prayer; it has a crown above and a Teutonic serpent from Anglian pre-Christian religion curves round the dial.

Entry is through the south porch, which today houses finds and Saxon carving. The nave has its orginal five high windows, square-headed on the north and round-headed on the south and in the west gable. The north-east window has a Roman inscription on the right jamb. Once all had horn-covered shutters. The crude font, still used, is shaped for the total immersion of infants. The sanctuary or chancel is entered beneath a tall re-assembled Róman arch with an Irish consecration cross incised beside it. Part of a 9th-century stone standing cross or grave cover stands behind the altar; the right jamb of the blocked north door is carved with Adam and Eve beside the Tree of Life; and the inserted 13th-century south lancet window jamb is a re-used Saxon stone etched similarly to grave memorials at Hartlepool.

In the 13th century two windows were added to admit more light: a tall lancet in the chancel, and another in the nave; the western annexe was demolished, and its stone was re-used to construct the south porch. Its sundial was a 17th-century addition. These, and 19th-century east and west windows and one in the nave, are the only changes to the Saxon building. A perceptive visitor will find a wealth of other detail.

LUMLEY CASTLE

The castle crowns a hill above the River Wear in pleasant parkland (6 miles north of Durham, 1 mile east of Chester-le-Street and close to the A1 (M)). The Castle, built in the 14th century with central courtyard and four great corner towers, incorporates Sir Ralph Lumley's earlier manor house as its west side. The original east entrance, flanked by angle-towers, overlooks the deep ravine of Lumley Beck. Richard Lumley, who became Earl of Scarbrough in 1689, planned alterations for which his son, in 1721, commissioned designs by Sir John Vanbrugh,

Lumley Castle: the south front. The castle welcomes families and conferences, besides specialising in Elizabethan banquets. (Tel: (0191) 389 1111.)

Northumbria Tourist Board.

including fine stuccoed decorations to walls and ceilings. The present earl is no longer resident and the castle was converted to a hotel in 1974. Lumley Castle welcomes families and conferences, besides specialising in Elizabethan banquets.

FINCHALE PRIORY

From 1196 Durham Priory had a cell here on the site of St Godric's hermitage (1115–70) where he died aged 106. In the 14th century it became a holiday house for Durham monks. A resident prior and four monks received groups of four others on successive 3-week visits. The considerable remains of church, cloister and other buildings from the mid-13th century are in the custody of English Heritage.

Finchale Priory: the ruins lie in picturesque woodland by the River Wear 5 miles north of Durham between the A1 and the A690. Open: Easter–end September. Adults £1.00, children under 16 50p, concessions 80p. Rest of year open but unattended, and admission free. (Tel: (0191) 386 3828 or (0191) 261 1585.)   *Durham County Council.*

WASHINGTON OLD HALL

Here, until 1452, lived the descendants of William de Wessyngton, direct ancestor of George Washington, first President of the U.S.A. The house was rebuilt about 1623.

Washington Old Hall: west end of the great hall, with part of the screens passage and two arches, features of the 14th-century house. Light refreshments. Hall and gardens open for weddings and receptions. National Trust. Open: 1 April to 30 October daily, except Thursday, Friday and Saturday (open Good Friday), 11 a.m. to 5 p.m., last admissions 4 p.m. Admissions: Adults £2·30; children £1·15; pre-booked parties of 15 or more £1·80. (Tel: (0191) 416 6879.)

Tyne and Wear County Council.

BEAMISH: NORTH OF ENGLAND OPEN AIR MUSEUM

Beamish: Pockerley Manor and Horse Yard, based on a medieval fortified manor house where costumed characters recreate the life and work of a yeoman farming family almost 200 years ago. Open: summer (April–end October) daily 10 a.m.–5 p.m.; winter (November–March) 10 a.m.–4 p.m., closed Mondays and Fridays. A winter visit is centred on the town and tramway; other areas are closed and consequently admission charges are reduced. Shop; restaurant; large free car park. For further information: write Beamish North of England Open Air Museum, Beamish, County Durham, DH9 0RG; or Tel: (0191) 231811.

Beamish is on A693, signposted from A1(M) Chester-le-Street exit, junction 63. The site covers 200 acres of beautiful county Durham countryside, and vividly illustrates life in the North of England in the early 1800s and 1900s. It has a drift mine, colliery village, Home Farm with traditional breeds of animals and poultry, railway station with rolling stock and signal box, a Methodist chapel, and a school. At Pockerley Manor, the life style of a yeoman family almost 200 years ago is recreated. Visitors take a tram ride to visit the town, with its shops, working pub, stables, garage, newspaper office, sweet factory, dentist's and other professional houses.

Beamish has won the distinction of being British Museum of the Year, and European Museum of the Year.

There is much else to see and do in the area.
Intending visitors should consult the *Leisure Map of Northumbria* published by the Northumbria Tourist Board.

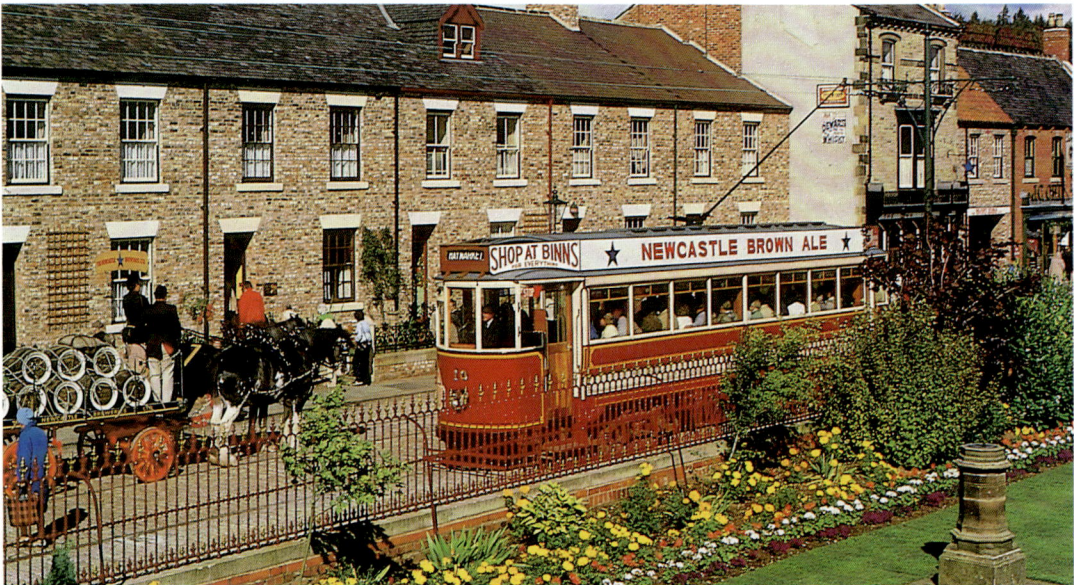

Beamish, the North of England Open Air Museum: part of the award-winning town.

First published, 1970   Second edition, 1974
Third edition, revised and rearranged with additions, 1982
Fourth edition, with colour photographs, 1983   Fifth edition, revised and with additions, 1987
Sixth edition, revised and with additions, 1992
Seventh edition, revised, with additions and new photographs, 1997
The text, newly revised and with additions, was previously published as Durham: a pictorial history and guide.
© Margot Johnson, 1970, 1974, 1982, 1983, 1987, 1992, 1997

Published by Turnstone Ventures, 37, Hallgarth Street, Durham, DH1 3AT
Designed and Printed by Beric Tempest, Great Britain, TR26 3HT. Telephone: (01736) 752500.

Martin G. Snape, Esq., M.A., kindly read the original text and made many helpful suggestions.

Back cover: **Durham Market Place:** Londonderry statue. *Claughton Photography.*